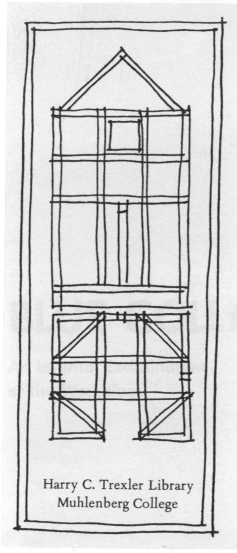

AR

BLUE COLLAR

an internal examination of the workplace

CHARLES SPENCER

Vanguard Books
Chicago, IL

First edition 1977 Lakeside-Charter Books
Second edition 1978 Vanguard Books
P.O. Box 3566
Chicago, IL 60654

Printed in the United States of America
Library of Congress Catalog Number: 76-50937
ISBN 0-917702-05-0

Grateful acknowledgement is made to Alfred A.
Knopf, Inc. for permission to reprint five lines
from the poem: "Dream Deferred" from THE
PANTHER AND THE LASH: POEMS OF
OUR TIMES, by Langston Hughes, copyright
1951 by Alfred A. Knopf, Inc.

For my beloved wife, Jean;
for Scott, Lisa, and Mike;
and for the workers in the plant
who I was privileged to represent.

"He who has access to the fountain does not go to the water-pot."

—*Leonardo da Vinci*

"In handicrafts and manufacture, the workman makes use of a tool; in the factory, the machine makes use of him . . ."

—*Karl Marx*

CONTENTS

Introduction

I THE PROPER STUDY OF THE BLUE COLLAR WORKER IS THE WORKPLACE

1.	Stalking the Blue Collar Worker	9
2.	Joe Magarac—Dead or Alive	20

II A BLUE COLLAR HERO IS SOMETHING TO BE

3.	Taking Sides	39
4.	A Right Arm for the Company	54
5.	Hard Core Unemployed	71
6.	Rank and File	86

III INSIDE COLLECTIVE BARGAINING

7.	Union Headquarters is Far from the Workplace	117
8.	Five Steps to Failure	134

IV THE WORKPLACE AND ITS DISCONTENTS

9.	Rigged!	145
10.	Nine Cents Ain't the World	155
11.	Can't Sell Out my Mind	167
12.	Is there a Doctor in the Workplace?	185
13.	The Blue Collar Apprentice— an Endangered Species	193
14.	Invoking Article Twelve	211
15.	The Toothless Tiger in the Coke Plant	219
16.	The Fingers, Arms, Legs, Balls and Carcasses of Blue Collar Workers Still Come at Bargain Prices	227

Epilogue

Introduction

This is a book about workers, not the go-for-broke vagabonds celebrated at folk festivals, nor those exceptional souls for whom work is an ascetic's reward or a revolutionary discipline, but, rather, about plain, obscure, everyday blue collar workers for whom work is the only choice, skilled, semi-skilled and unskilled, and how they make it in the workplace: their daily hassles over working conditions, their beefs and grievances against the boss, their union loyalties and frustrations, their personal reactions to occupational hazards, their struggles with racial and ethnic discrimination, their periodic encounters with the work ethic, their irrepressible demands for a better life. Who and what is the blue collar worker? Is the blue collar worker disappearing, as some social theorists contend?

The book is also about bosses, not the Chamber of Commerce or the Harvard School of Business rendition, but, rather, the authentic management people in the hierarchy of the workplace, upholding and defending company policies, checking, recording, and cleverly forgetting if required, exercising a wide range of authority over the workers, maintaining discipline, artfully using the carrot and the stick, making the tough decisions on enforcement of the union contract (where it exists), keeping the works running at a profit.

It is also about labor unions—local unions, international officials, dissident rank and file movements—and how they relate to the blue collar workers: their internal procedures, their agreements and disputes with the employers, their agreements and disputes with their own members, their patterns of collective bargaining, their role in restraining the workers. Does collective bargaining really work? Are unions in bed with the companies? Are they in firm control of their members? How many miles and moons is it from the international headquarters in Washington and Pittsburgh to the workplaces in South Chicago and Detroit?

Far too many studies of the blue collar workers of America have become bogged down and consumed in a lavish feast of academic speculation from which the blue collar workers themselves have been routinely excluded or ignored. There are virtually no published books about the worker inside the workplace. Though it may come off as sort of simplistic, and not particularly epigramatic, this book is based on the conviction that *the proper study of the blue collar worker is the workplace.* No matter what other institutions are searched for prints or clews all trails lead back to the workplace itself—not the tavern, not the university, not the census tracts, or what is recorded on interviewers' tapes, not the pool hall, Legion or K. of C. halls, not even the union hall. Unless it is fully grasped that these are synthetic settings, not of their own making, and, in a sense lures and traps or escapes, which remove the blue collar workers from their natural habitat, one can easily run wild in accounting for and analyzing the blue collar workers. The qualities of the blue collar worker go far deeper than where most blue collar studies have been inclined to search. There's no denying, of course, that institutions other than the workplace have influenced the blue collar worker, and that the workers have, in turn, as have other groups, exerted their own unique influence on these institutions. But studies of the blue collar worker shouldn't confuse effects with causes. (In a quite parallel situation, it took a popular civil rights revolution before Black studies in America became bold enough to look beyond the urban ghettos and other white-made institutions, and to research the African origins of Blacks in America.)

Who would put up with a study of foot soldiers partitioned off from the battlefield, or of school teachers secluded from the classroom, or of medical doctors shut out from the hospitals and laboratories? Yet, in the studies of the blue collar worker, the workplace, where the blue collar workers spend the greatest part of their lives, doesn't seem to rate an examination.

In this respect, this book departs from the surveys, interviews, polls, sociological studies, union profiles, political projections and other eye-catching comments being presented to satisfy the current public curiosity about work and the blue collar worker.

The approach here is that any and all definitions, symbols, portrayals, statements, examples, tables and theories of blue collar workers, must be tested out on the proving grounds of the workplace. If it won't hold up there, it's probably phony.

As an example, when a distinguished interviewer-writer presented a "typical" steelworker, who, in the quiet of his living room, confessed to the humming tape-recorder that "I got no use for intellectuals, but I want my kid to be an effete snob," where, other than in the hot glow of the mill-furnace and in the full view of the mill workers, can such literary featherbedding be tested? It's past time to shed the familiar stereotypes, the ersatz proletarians, the chic implications, and other nonsense that is being passed off as "blue collar studies", and, instead of the staged, self-conscious, environment, professionally set up by investigators, it is necessary to focus directly on the blue collar workers in their common, everyday, unstaged work environment.

This book is not a "study" in the sense that observations,

reports and documents are systematically and precisely labeled, numbered, and summarized, following the method of the conventional university scholar. The decision to reject this method is mainly a reaction to the scholastic violence committed against the blue collar workers over the centuries, and also that the author is not a conventional scholar—as the prim reader may easily detect—but is, himself, a blue collar worker.

Nor can this book be considered an autobiography, even with its author having participated quite intimately in all the affairs and experiences presented. There was a period in the course of writing this book that it had a tentative title "My Twenty-Five Years in Steel," but the scope of the book underwent a major change. In response to what the author recognized as a more urgent need of the times, the book developed, purposefully, into a more objective and detailed account of the blue collar workers, separating, but not concealing, the author's own feelings and judgments concerning their experiences in the workplace, staying clear of any temptations to prophesize the future of Labor in America.

The experiences of the workers described here are not the private affairs one might confide to their psychiatrist or chaplain or broker. Neither are they composites or fictions to bolster a social theory or construct a literary piece. They are public affairs in the sense that they happened in full view of witnesses and other interested workers, and they happened exactly in the manner described here, and are readily recognized by most blue collar workers as average, everyday events, which occur on any workday. (In several instances the names of individuals have been changed, because they've had enough trouble and wouldn't want the attention publication of their names might bring.)

Though this book is based, principally, in one steel plant (the South Chicago works of Republic Steel Corporation), it is not misleading to consider this plant a microcosm that reflects the universal truths of the workplace of America. A steel mill has a broad mix of occupations and workers, skilled, semi-skilled and unskilled; Black, white, Latinos; ethnics and WASPs; precision workers and assembly-line workers; back-breaking labor and light machine work; outside and inside work; transporting, shipping, fabrication, forging, smelting, constructing; simple mechanical and sophisticated computerized processes; it's all there in an integrated steel plant such as the works in South Chicago.

The obvious advantage in focusing on one single plant is that it can make up in depth what it loses in breadth (a technique so successful in Lynd's classic, *Middletown*). Twenty-five years in one plant seems to be about right and more to the point than random hitches of a couple of months or years in several different plants—unless one is interested in the story of a drifter. Plant seniority still is a treasured blue collar asset, and the views and reactions of a blue collar worker with long service generally carry more weight than those of a summer employee who is experimenting or trying to get enough money for fall tuition.

It is common knowledge that, except for those blue collar industries closely related to women's traditional household chores (clothing, cleaning, cooking), and those lower-paid jobs in light assembly and marginal businesses, women have been, until very recently, systematically shut out from blue collar jobs in the major industries of America. Women's entrance into blue collar jobs previously considered the exclusive dominion of the male has profoundly affected the character of the workplace, the trade union, and workingclass culture. But this social phenomenon has been universally evaded, as if, somehow, it would soon fade away like Rosie the Riveter of the World War II era. As long as middle-class and upper-class women remain the chief spokespersons of women's liberation, the woman blue collar worker is bound to suffer from misrepresentation in the same manner as her blue collar brothers. There is no plan in this book, because it is beyond the first-hand experience of its writer, to tell the story of the blue collar woman-worker. This exciting project is waiting for a spirited daughter of Labor, probably recently hired, on a basic oxygen furnace, an auto assembly line, a Pennsylvania coal mine, a transcontinental carrier, an urban construction site, or any blue collar job—and here, because it is critical, we may have to settle for one with less than twenty-five years seniority.

The writing of this book began in earnest when one of the foremen in the mechanical department of the rolling mills passed along the word that all employees with twenty-five years service (that included this writer) were "to get their asses over to the superintendent's office," to have their pictures taken and receive a pin-set. Though it frequently happens in smaller plants, this was the first time in this plant's history that the workers were given any such recognition. The ceremonies were being performed during working hours, so they had to be done quickly. No chance to change clothes or wash the grime off your face. No drinks, no back-slapping, no speeches. Just click-click and the flash of the camera, and the embarrassed distribution of brooches studded with tiny anonymous stones. Everyone was grateful for the minutes off from work and the chance to sit down in an air-conditioned superintendent's office. But, after twenty-five years, there should have been more, don't you think? Even more than this book attempts.

The Proper Study of the Blue Collar Worker Is the Workplace

Chapter One

Stalking the Blue Collar Worker

The profound interest in what's on the mind of the blue collar worker these days has surfaced a prominent and aggressive group of social engineers, pollsters, interviewers, government investigators, and researchers of varied motives and interests, briskly engaged in stalking the blue collar workers of America. However, in all this activity, and in all the documentaries and evaluations and findings, it is notable that the blue collar workers themselves have seldom, if ever, been allowed to talk back, to tell their own story.

Soldiers, industry tycoons, half-backs, hookers, lawyers and felons have all but produced a literary glut. They are routinely seen and heard on television and radio. But the blue collar worker has been wordless and faceless and indifferent, allowing others, plugged in as authorities, coordinators or spokesmen, to tell the blue collar story—clearly a tragedy that is responsible for the blue collar worker's profile being knotted in so many contradictions.

Some scholars and researchers, aspiring to edge closer to the blue collar worker, to have a dialogue of a sort with them, and to elevate the quality of "blue collar studies", have hit upon the oral interview and the tape recorder as the magic instrument to conjure the truth from the blue collar worker.

But how does the professional, bent on studying the world of work, break through the blue collar workers' deep-seated mistrust of investigators? Is it surprising that they suspect they are being hustled when even the most charming interviewer solicits their views about matters which they have never before been consulted? And that their responses are guarded, or geared to what they conceive to be the fixed rules of the game? Give 'em what they want.

One of the earliest and most celebrated studies to measure the blue collar workers' reactions to conditions in the workplace was the "Hawthorne Study", conducted by the Harvard School of Business, funded by the Rockefeller Foundation. It was directed by the Western Electric Company, a subsidiary of the American Telephone and Telegraph Company, at its Hawthorne plant in Cicero, Illinois. Groups of Hawthorne employees were studied over a five year period, from 1927 to 1932, to determine the effects of changing working conditions on the employees' *productivity*. (No matter what lofty aims are publicly announced, and regardless of their humanitarian affectations, the real target of blue collar studies, throughout the decades, has been greater production at lower labor costs. Even social reformers most solidly devoted to the working class are often, at the same time, firm supporters of higher productivity—perhaps to make commodities less expensive for the poor.)

The big question at Hawthorne and other workplaces at that time was whether making workers more comfortable and relaxed during work, and exhibiting an interest in the workers' mental and emotional problems, would result in greater productivity. Management teams encouraged the workers to "talk out their problems." What did they want the company to do to make them happier at work? Did they want better lighting. Did they want to work at piece rates rather than hourly rates. Did they want to start work earlier, and quit later? How was it at home? Did they have problems with their spouses or parents? The management teams listened carefully, and responded to the workers' suggestions for changes. And then the workers' output was measured. Dr. Sigmund Freud's fame in America, initially popularized in the penthouses, was now pragmatically penetrating the workplaces.

The "Hawthorne Study" is regarded a landmark in the nation's inquiry into the world of the blue collar worker. Every high school student of social studies learns that when the lighting was better the Hawthorne workers showed their appreciation by producing more. (In fact, it wasn't that way. No matter how the company changed conditions—more lighting, less lighting, piece work, day work, changes in temperature, and humidity, personal counseling, removing or adding any number of working conditions, and finally right back to the very same conditions in effect before the experiment began—the workers under the control experiment, illogically, produced more than the normal 2400 relays a week.)

The fiftieth anniversary of the "Hawthorne Study" observed at a symposium in Chicago heard Dr. Albert Morrow, president of the National Academy of Professional Psychologists, deliver a eulogy, noting that "industry has not learned the lesson that humanized treatment of employees produce better workers"—not a remarkable observation for a psychology academy.

The Roper Research organization, some twenty years after Hawthorne, conducted the bench-mark survey of workers, covering sixteen different blue collar industries. It's findings, published in *Fortune Magazine* are still regarded as Holy Writ wherever blue collar studies are marketed.

"Is your job too simple to bring out your best abilities, or not?"

That's one of the bombs the Roper survey dropped on the workers.

For ages blue collar workers have been hustled by morale

engineers and time and motion men snooping around their machines and workbenches with stop watches and clip boards, obviously bent on a plan to add more work to the jobs. Workers have learned how to handle these people, and the unwritten rule is to tell them nothing—not even the right time.

Other samples in the Roper survey: *"Does your job leave you tired at the end of the day, or not?"*

"Is your kind of job where someone would have to take your place if you had to leave your work?"

"Is your job really essential to the success of the Company?"

"Can you do the work on your job and keep your mind on other things most of the time?"

Blue collar workers know so well that these are the questions and these are the people that can do them in . . . that the Company has trained these bird-dogs . . . that they are on a hunt to eliminate them and their job . . . or that it's a con-game to speed-up the job . . . "well, my mother didn't raise dummies, so fuck you."

A professional pollster's devastating affair with the steelworkers is a classical illustration of the occupational hazards in the business of interviewing blue collar workers. Indeed it may have been the major factor which finally plunged the industry into the long and bitter national steel strike of 1959. The destructive role of this poll during the strike has never been acknowledged either by the union or the steel corporations.

The highly reputable public opinion pollster, Samuel Lubell, reported that the results of his interviews with steelworkers at the plant gates throughout the country showed that they were overwhelmingly opposed to a strike that was being threatened by their union leaders, and that they would not support the strike. These findings, headlined in all the steel communities, fitted perfectly into the calculations that were guiding the steel industry executives, who had always inclined to the doctrine that steelworkers, under the right conditions, could be weaned away from their union. Yes, they would take on the union, and once and for all bring to an end the union's interference with management's rights to run the works. The poll confirmed that this was the right time.

It is now history that the Lubell poll, failing to ask the right questions, didn't get the right answers from the steelworkers. With the expiration of the contract, the International officers of the steelworkers union, themselves scared stiff by the poll, and in a tight squeeze, were obliged to declare a strike. The workers, contrary to the poll, gave the strike call spontaneous and enthusiastic support. The strike lasted 116 days—the longest in the history of the industry. The militancy of the strike confounded the steelmasters, and the officials of the union were slow to understand the feelings of their union members. (The issue was "featherbedding", and the workers recognized it as a code-word for speed-up, unemployment and reduction of earnings.) It's a well-known secret that the president of the International Union, during the entire period of the strike suffered from vague, disabling, symptoms and the contract negotiations were handled by lesser union officials and attorneys.

After 116 days of strike, industry leaders, somewhat disenchanted with the professional pollsters, sniffed out a more reliable assessment of the steelworkers' state of mind from reports of their foremen and supervisors in the plants who were closer to the workers. They gave up their war against the union and signed a contract without any specific provision for eliminating featherbedding.

There hasn't been a strike in the steel industry since 1959. But if it again reaches that point, steelworkers would probably appreciate an apology rather than a poll from blue collar researchers.

It was reported in Volume 38 of *Public Opinion Quarterly* by researchers Charles Weaver and Carol Swanson that a sample of 339 firemen and policemen in San Antonio, Texas, when surveyed, gave untruthful answers. Thirty-six percent lied about their rank, and less than one percent gave truthful information about their salaries (checked against the official records of the city.) How naive to suppose that Texan firemen or policemen would confide in Eastern Establishment interviewing companies!

In late December, 1975, the day after the Gallup Poll showed Gerald Ford would win an election over Hubert Humphrey, the Harris poll came out with its poll showing the very opposite. A few more such misadventures, and all polls, not only those dealing with blue collar workers, could lose their tyrannical hold on the public mind.

Many students and researchers in "blue collar studies", allowing for the flaws in the oral interview, have adopted a more direct technique. They have changed their shirts from dacron to denim, disguised themselves in other ways, even changing their names for a period, and secured jobs in factories and workshops. They moved into blue collar neighborhoods, frequented their taverns, and lived the lives of blue collar workers. The initial example of this technique took place more than fifty years ago. Whiting Williams, then personnel director of the Hydraulic Pressed Steel Company, left his post and went to work in another steel mill for several months as a laborer under an assumed name. With a trained eye, keeping careful notes, he studied the steelworkers while pretending to be one of them. He published his observations in a book called *What's On the Worker's Mind: By One Who Put On Overalls to Find Out.* Though the author-turned-worker acknowledged that he probably didn't fool many workers and that his newly cultivated comrades spotted him for a "spy", his book had a powerful influence on the academic community—a novel success story in the stalking of the blue collar worker.

A kind of sequel to Mr. Williams' story was recently produced by the president of Philadelphia's Haverford College. John R. Coleman spent a portion of his sabbatical leave in the disguise of a blue collar worker. His book, *Blue Collar Journal*, tells how he got a job digging sewers in Atlanta (you can't get more blue collar than that!) and stuck with it for two weeks. His next job, more white-collarish, was a dishwasher in Boston, and he relates how he was charitably fired before he finished the day. This was followed by a job as a salad-man in a Boston oyster house. After a couple of weeks, still uncorrupted by the managerial functions which had attached to his salad-man's job, he hired in as a garbage collector in the Washington suburb of Silver Spring, Maryland. These four blue collar jobs during three months of a sabbatical leave from his presidential office at Haverford (during which he also managed to squeeze in regular meetings of the board of directors of a bank) are hardly grounds for claiming expertise on the blue collar workers of America. (In all fairness, Mr. Coleman makes no such claim, even if his publisher does.)

In 1972, a bolder and more vigorous plan for stalking the blue collar worker was fathered by the Students for a Democratic Society (SDS) and other radically oriented youth groups. They decided to "colonize" the workplace, to join the workers' trade unions, to become activists in the plants, and to lead the blue collar workers in the revolution. Not a three month or six months trip, but for as long as it may be required to reach the promised land. So serious a threat was this considered by industry, that the Commerce and Industry Association called a meeting of industrial managers to discuss "guerrilla warfare" in the workplace. Union officials also held meetings, and worked out a joint labor-management strategy "to smoke out these infiltrators." The *Fairless Union News* declared, "Their purpose is to cause trouble."

Many of the "colonizers" persevered long enough to be interviewed by academic researchers or to participate on television talk shows as genuine blue collar workers, some joined rank and file movements within their local unions, some became labor experts within revolutionary sects and delivered position papers at their conventions. Most of them, early in their worklife, became disheartened and disgusted with what they diagnosed as workers' indifference to their exploitation and to their bourgeois outlook on life. "I'm sick of coddling the workers," confided a youthful colonizer at Republic Steel in South Chicago. "If you can't make a revolution in a year," he said, tugging on his Christ-like beard, "you may as well quit the mill."

(Colonizing of industry for purposes other than making a living was not invented by the SDS. It was done with middling success by the American Federation of Labor, the CIO, Socialist and Communist organizers from their very early beginnings.)

The strike at the General Motors plant in Lordstown, Ohio, in 1972, roused the strongest imaginable juices of the entire mafia of blue collar ideologues. At last, it was here! The three week strike of 8000 workers, which included a conspicuous number of colonizers active in the local UAW union, was euphemistically christened the "Lordstown Rebellion," and was linked, impertinently, with the Paris Commune of 1871. It was swiftly analyzed as a strike against the Work Ethic, against monotony in the workplace, against the assembly line, and the signal for a nationwide strike of the workingclass. "Lordstown" still hangs on as a code word, breathlessly whispered among the constituents of America's counter culture, years after its youthful leaders had moved on to other, less adventurous, pursuits within the establishment.

Immediately following the Lordstown strike, there appeared the 1972 federal government report, *Work in America*, and H.E.W. study, under the direction of then-Undersecretary Elliot L. Richardson. It charged that industry and government are woefully ignorant about blue collar workers (which nobody would dispute) and proceeded to embrace almost every fiction and myth of that fantastic community that dominates blue collar studies. *Work in America* managed to recruit them all as either authors, consultants or quotable authorities. There are, inevitably, Bell and Bluestone and Chinoy, Garson, Ginsberg, O'Toole, Roche, Sexton, Wurf; and some "outsiders" too—the Johnny-come-latelys of blue collar studies: *Newsweek*, Senator Percy, and the *Wall Street Journal*.

Work in America is stuffed full with baleful references to "worker's alienation," their "attraction towards extremist social and political movements," their propensity for "sabotage [as] a way of asserting individuality in a homogeneous world," (whew!), their "hostility towards the government," the "breakdown of the work ethic"—all out of the repertoire of the Lordstown Rebellion guerrilla theatre. Not one bona fide blue collar worker had a hand in the report.

Was this the common variety of confusion one generally encounters in blue collar studies? Or was it a studied government effort to shake up the smug upper classes of our Republic? Or perhaps a Nixon provocation of the sort uncorked at Watergate?

All that is certain is that the Report was never followed up and has been forgotten. But at the time it cleared the way for the most fantastic "discoveries" about blue collar workers. A headline in the *New York Times* on May 26, 1973, said: GE WORKERS UPSTATE ARE DISCONTENTED WITH WORK ITSELF. That's the ultimate! As far as you can go in recording the collapse of our system.

The news story quoted a dozen or so employees of the GE plant in Schenectady. Their remarks left little doubt that the workingclass of America was preparing to pull up stakes and take off for a commune somewhere in New Mexico.

A red-bearded operator told the reporter, "No, I don't like this work. Not really. There's lots of heavy lifting . . . we got problems with supervisors who bird-dog you all day long."

A young GE worker named Ryan Henry said he would rather be racing stock cars than working, but he needed a few thousand dollars to build a competitive car, and that's the reason he was still working.

A GE chipper and grinder said that the work was tiring, "but it beats walking the streets to find something to do."

Other workers were reported to have ripped into the very

fabric of blue collar work, and the *New York Times*—not the *Village Voice*—made the gloomy diagnosis, seasonally popular in '73, that the work system was indeed critically sick, sick, sick. For a period, discussions of "blue collar blues" crowded out articles on VD in the Sunday supplements.

While small controlled doses of griping may be perceived as a shrewd procedure for preserving the health of the system, promiscuous injections by unlicensed quacks are something else. Things obviously were getting out of hand. A group of certified medical doctors from Rutgers Medical College in New Jersey arrived in the nick of time, to make a no-nonsense survey of 1026 auto assembly-line workers at the General Motors plant in the Baltimore area. They came up with findings quite different from what was discovered at the GE plant in Schenectady, or what was reported by the United States government task force in *Work in America*. The doctors found that *ninety-five percent of the GM workers said they were satisfied with their jobs.* Seventy-one percent said no part of their work was tiring or boring. The doctors found that those workers who did experience depression or dissatisfaction are those "who would be considered emotionally disturbed" and are definitely a minority of the blue collar workers. The survey was written up in the February 1974 issue of *Archives of General Psychiatry,* published by the American Medical Association.

The Wall Street Journal, quickly switched its endorsement to the "positive" findings of Rutgers University, in preference to the "negative" GE reports of the *New York Times*. It also retracted its support of the U.S. government's blue collar study, and editorialized that "a good many interpreters took workers' gripes and complaints far too seriously."

One can only guess how much the blue collar workers of America have been internally influenced by the pursuits of the bungling pollsters, disoriented colonizers, hustling publishers, alienated professors of social sciences, or self-serving government boards. But it would be a mistake to suppose the blue collar workers could somehow be changed or converted or redeemed by the efforts of these "outsiders", as if a blue collar worker were some kind of cult or league, that, by a show of hands or a vote can change its by-laws or rituals, or like an ethnic group could be absorbed or blended into a common melting pot. It is, of course, the working conditions and rules and union agreements and class conflicts and the economics of the workplace itself that genuinely molds and shapes the blue collar workers.

Chapter Two

Joe Magarac—Dead or Alive

There is a widely held belief in our land, buttressed by statistical tables, census tracts and demographic experts, that the blue collar workers are rapidly dwindling away. Not just out of the public's view, in the manner of Michael Harrington's "invisible poor," or that the blue collar worker has been converted to the counter-culture, or has been completely won over to the bourgeoisie—though this argument too has gained popularity—but that they have been wiped out of existence, totally and irrevocably, as if an earthquake had devoured them.

The announcement of this extraordinary shift in the social order has quite universally been accepted, and in surprisingly many circles it has been greeted as a fair and just restraint upon a recalcitrant sector of society.

The idea of cutting the blue collar workers down to size—of shaping and molding them to fit the needs of the system, so they'll know who's boss, of skillfull use of the carrot and stick, of disciplines, lay-offs and discharges, of all the work-rules and economic controls applied in the workplace—is nothing new. It's the established formula for getting "a fair day's work for a fair day's pay", which is written into most labor agreements between the unions and corporations.

In many circles of society today, the blue collar worker is placed in the same bracket of "undesirables" with Blacks, Indians, Puerto Ricans, or any group one feels guilty about. Dalton Trumbo, the black-listed liberal Hollywood writer, revered for his courageous stand for freedom of thought, is quoted as saying, "I've never considered the workingclass anything other than something to get out of." Except during political elections, social upheavals, or war, when they are critically needed for support, the blue collar worker is rejected as a misfit in society, a loser, somebody you wouldn't want your sister (or brother) to marry.

In the earlier half of the twentieth century, both in the cities and rural areas of America, a popular non-physical pastime was for kinsmen and parochial mates to gather after work, or school, or household chores, at bars, fraternity houses, store-steps, or panelled basements, and confide in one another about the vehemence of their dislike for Blacks and Jews, and, in some regions, Catholics, ethnics, and radicals. (Chicanos and Indians had not yet arrived.) It is said that hate is endemic in America, historically sealed in its colonial birth, nursed in the schools and churches, that it is married to the state and never stops seeking new victims. There are, of course, fashions and styles and seasons for hate. Everyone knows that in these times it isn't fashionable, and could even be dangerous, to make remarks about "niggers", or "kikes", or "hunkies", or even "ethnic purity." But it seems "open season" on blue collar workers never comes to a close.

Blue collar workers, with their outrageous demands for higher and higher wages—they're holding a gun to the head of the American consumer! That's all it takes to get the middle-class juices flowing.

Imagine an electrician, or plumber or steelworker getting ten dollars an hour!

Blue collar workers take no pride in their work, they cheat

on the job, loaf and never get anything done. It's an outrage.

The frequent break-down of automobiles, dishwashers, dryers, expressways, trains, is because of workers' sabotage.

Bolts aren't tightened, seams and joints aren't welded, bearings aren't greased, electrical wires aren't properly spliced, and the iron rots away—all because of the blue collar workers' orneriness.

Illinois U.S. Senator Charles Percy, with an eye on the anti-blue collar voters, delivered a vehement speech to Congress, inserted into the *Congressional Record,* about his horrendous experience with a spanking new Detroit-made automobile he was driving to attend a constituent's funeral. The car fell apart. From the battery to the rear end, part after part collapsed. He never made it to the funeral. Sabotage? Skulduggery? Subversion? You name it.

Remember the tragic fire of 1967 that killed three astronauts in their Apollo space capsule? A Congressional investigation of the accident reported it was caused by "the shoddy workmanship of welders, electricians, and other craftsmen." This was the first recognition blue collar workers had ever received in the space program. It was always believed only Ph.Ds and the military elite were engaged in space.

A 1976 accident involving two rapid transit trains meeting head-on in Chicago, injuring several hundred commuters, roused up the former U.S. congressman, Alderman Pucinski, and before any other politician could get the jump on him, he put the finger on the CTA workers, charging them with negligence and drunkenness. The alderman offered no apology when the CTA management admitted to the malfunctioning of the signalling apparatus, and the lack of safety equipment.

Example on top of example can be cited to illustrate this brand of contempt for and victimization of the blue collar worker. The public's appetite for such fare seems insatiable.

It is sometimes assumed there is a natural affinity between Blacks and the blue collar workers of America. Not exactly so, if one were to search the list of persons honored at the

"Awards Dinner of Black Achievers" in Chicago's Conrad Hilton hotel on November 12, 1975. The dinner, sponsored by the YMCA was announced as a way of paying tribute "to those Blacks who are making it on the job, as opposed to businessmen or professionals." It would seem here was an occasion to cite Black steelworkers who have advanced to melters (it's rumored there are two in the area), Black aircraft workers who are master mechanics, Black construction workers who helped put together the Sears Tower, Black seamstresses who have become designers, Black policemen who have a way with the kids.

Of the one hundred and thirty-nine Black "achievers" honored, there were salesmen, publishers, bank employees, accountants, one union official, administrators, journalists—all professionals—but not one solitary blue collar worker. Where has the YMCA been all these years to assume the Black community had not been contaminated with the mischievous antiblue collar virus? Even the AFL-CIO honors only those workers who have climbed into elevated management, government or union positions—never a worker who's humping it on the assembly-line.

At the beginning of the century, a steel mill superintendent was quoted as saying, "Gorilla men are what is needed in the steel industry." In a society that was fixed in its destiny to build an industrial empire, the steelworker as a gorilla man probably didn't strike as that outrageous a thought. That image of a steelworker, or any blue collar worker hasn't remarkably changed. It is common for the blue collar worker to be represented in literature, stage, television, paintings, as someone untamed, animalistic, simple-minded, uncouth.

The "gorilla man" was later replaced with a more ethnic figure, more representative of the new workers from southern and eastern Europe who began pouring into the workplaces. *Joe Magarac* became the mythical folk hero of the mills.

Children of steel workers learn in school about the exploits of *Joe Magarac* and identify more readily than they can with

Beowulf. In the mills, steelworkers of special brawn who worked furiously to out-do their fellow-workers and win favor with their bosses, were good-naturedly nicknamed *Joe Magarac.* It was said *Joe Magarac* was seven feet tall, born from the womb of an ore mine, and made out of steel. He was in perpetual competition with all his buddies in the mill, making work a game, and winning every time. He laughed uproariously at the puny muscles of the others, as he squeezed hot molten steel through the fingers of his spectacularly powerful hands to shape rails for the Union Pacific, girders for the Flatiron Building, plate for the steamboat ferries. He worked with such speed, that one day the mill ran out of steel, and *Joe Magarac*, totally devoted to the Protestant Work Ethic, without losing a split second, dismembered his own massive body and hurled it into a ladle of boiling steel.

Now, that's a real worker. *Joe Magarac.* (*Magarac* is the Slavic word for *jackass.*)

From "gorilla man" to "jackass" wasn't a long leap. It was still within the range of beasts, reserved for those with proper license to hunt down. (A Papal Bull, declaring the Indians of Mexico to be animals that could be butchered, preceded the Spanish conquest. There were periods, too, in the U.S.A., like those of the Molly Maguires, Haymarket Square, Ludlow, Homestead, Memorial Day 1937, when it was "open season" to destroy blue collar workers who strayed from the fold.)

During the great depression of the 1930s the status of the blue collar worker suffered its worst humiliation. Out of work, they were marked as bums, tramps, moochers, social outcasts. Without savings or other resources, untrained in matters of politics and economics, as soon as they lost a single week's work they were in desperate circumstances. On the other hand, the unemployed white collar worker, bookkeeper, manager, or civil service worker had several natural advantages. Their higher salaries often gave them a chance to accumulate some savings. Or they could make purchases on credit, or borrow from friends or relatives. They weren't visibly poor, and they usually didn't become a burden on the community.

It was a common practice in large-scale industry to provide blue collar workers with one or two days of work a month, to make them ineligible for jobless aid. Two days in a plant, after carfare, work clothing, and other expenses, usually left the worker with less money than would have been received on welfare if totally unemployed. But to refuse would have meant loss of job as well as removal from the welfare rolls.

Reacting to critics, that the unemployed were being pampered on public aid, work projects (WPA) were set up during the Roosevelt New Deal administration, directed by social workers pleased to consider themselves liberals. But blue collar workers, regardless of their trades or skills, former mechanics, electricians, textile weavers, house painters, carpenters, were assigned to work on "pick and shovel projects," at wages providing no more than public welfare. On the other hand, unemployed professionals, intellectuals, accountants, and people from higher level positions in public and private industry, were assigned to pretentious, non-productive, fleeting, and often non-existing jobs in the arts, education, theater and social research, at salaries two and three times that of the pick and shovel workers. (This is not to demean the talented works of a number of these cultural projects.)

The full story of the blue collar worker in the Great Depression has never been told, nor, for that matter, has that entire history, as it relates to our later political, economic and social development, been digested. It has been virtually blacked out. Cliches, inventions, evasions, and downright falsifications have been panned off as gospel in accounting for this most embarrassing upheaval in the growth of the American system. People today live in unbelievable fear that a similar or even a more serious depression may erupt at any moment, and that there may be no second chance for recovery.

One of these cliches—that "*everyone had it rough* during the depression"—just doesn't hold up. The blue collar worker had it the *roughest*. (It may be legitimately argued that

Blacks and southern white tenant farmers were at a lower rung on the economic ladder, but at that time, they were the blood-brothers of the blue collar workers.) Many were not at all hurt by the Depression, and even became more affluent because of it. Because things were cheap, (and that's not a cliche) anyone with money was rich and could live in royal style. Sturdy teen-age daughters of Pennsylvania coal miners were recruited at wages "in kind" (board and room—no monetary pay) as servants, housemaids, cooks, nurses and varied other duties in the kitchens and boudoirs of Philadelphia, New York and Boston families for whom Depression was equated with Opportunity.

The tales of wealthy corporate directors and bankers jumping out of twenty-story windows in the Wall Street crash were highly exaggerated. The rich weren't ruined. It was the gamblers and newcomers to the world of finance that were crushed. The authentic rich continued to direct their affairs with a sharp nose for a profit.

Stories of creditors carrying their jobless customers on their books through the long years of depression may have been true for their favored patrons, but not for blue collar customers. As soon as it became evident that the workplaces weren't re-opening, they were cut off from further credit for food, fuel, clothing, housing. They even lost their welcome at church when they weren't able to drop a coin in the collection plate. When they couldn't pay their rent, they were thrown out of their homes like defeated civilians at the hands of conquering troops. The sidewalks in workingclass city blocks were cluttered with the furniture of the dispossessed.

Law enforcement agencies sadistically prayed upon the unemployed blue collar workers. When, in desperation, they took to the road in search of work in some other mythical state where jobs were rumored more plentiful, they were arrested for vagrancy. They were jailed, or, in states stubbornly committed to the work ethic, impressed into chain-gangs.

Even prisoners of war, protected by the Geneva Convention, received better treatment.

Though the blue collar workers were not totally passive in this long, ravaging economic crisis which reduced them to utter pauperism, their resistance, viewed in perspective, was pitifully faint-hearted. Contrary to popular mythology, there is no evidence that the ruling circles lost any sleep over fears they would be toppled by a revolution. The "New Deal" government was at all times well in control. The workers were poorly prepared for any kind of effective movement to bring about any fundamental change in the social order. They had no organization, there were no natural leaders for such a movement, and they had great difficulty in translating the appeals of Marxism in terms of their own life experiences. What there was of the trade unions had nothing whatsoever to offer the unemployed, and in most instances turned their backs on them. Probably nobody in America today believes workers would put up with such a depression again, just as hardly anyone believes the people of Germany would again consent to the gas chambers.

When, in the late 1930s, United States industry began to recover, and the blue collar workers were recalled to their jobs to build the materials of war, a long-delayed movement for reform was reflected in the phenomenal growth of the trade unions in the mills, mines and workplaces of America. This period of union organization, militant strikes of masses of workers, and political activism, was, by any measure, the blue collar workers' most triumphant hour. There developed a new appreciation for the role of the blue collar worker. Anti-labor laws were relaxed, and for the first time workers in mass production industries were allowed a measure of legal protection in organizing industrial unions.

Substantial sections of the community of intellectuals, students and middle class, chastened by the devastation of the Great Depression and what appeared to be a spread of Fascism in the country, saw the Labor Movement as their own cause, and supported it with funds, personnel, defense, and wherever it was accepted, an ideology. The democratic coalition of workers, middle class, and intellectuals, was being formed in support of the New Deal. Workers art, proletarian poetry, murals suggestive of workers' power, the rediscovery of Joe Hill and other labor martyrs, under the impetus of the burgeoning union movement was appearing in the most unlikely places.

But with all that seeming progress, the Joe Magarac, gorilla man, image of the blue collar worker hardly retreated. The old French axiom which says the more things change, the more they remain the same, seemed to hold with a vengeance.

The federal laws allowing workers the right to unionize simply weren't taken seriously by many employers and government agencies. It was an every-day occurrence for workers' picket-lines, parades, and organizing acitivities to be gunned down either by quasi-legal anti-labor groups or law enforcement agencies.

In Chicago, the police maintained an unofficial command post inside the Republic Steel plant in South Chicago, and let loose with gunfire, tear gas and clubs, killing ten workers and wounding ninety in a union parade in 1937. This was only one of the many scores of such violent attacks to warn blue collar workers not to get out of line.

The Memorial Day Massacre in Chicago was accorded less public notice (measured by column inches in the press) than the St. Valentine's Day Massacre that took place at a garage on North Clark Street in the same city, involving two rival gangs of the crime syndicate. There were fewer casualties on St. Valentine's day, but they weren't Joe Magaracs. They were successful businessmen of a sort, men smart enough to avoid the mills. When, in 1967, that garage was razed, collectors snatched up the bricks. But a recent effort to have a state or city historical marker placed at the scene of the Memorial Day massacre was blocked by both state and city government.

They saw no advantage in conceding that the killings may have been a mistake. (It is interesting that the intellectuals who, in the reign of McCarthy terrorism, were blacklisted for supporting the workers' battles, have been "rehabilitated" and restored to their previous or even higher status, but no move has yet been made to rehabilitate or memorialize the martyred blue collar workers and their families.)

With World War II the upgrading of the blue collar worker was destined. The battle of production became a patriotic cause, and it was not lost on the blue collar workers that they had become "essential." Conditions in the workplaces improved. Discipline relaxed. Overtime was abundant. A blue collar worker could save a buck, get credit, buy a car. People with money to spend are always treated with respect.

And then it was enthusiastically observed in some learned circles that the wartime prosperity had catapulted the blue collar workers into the middle class. No more Magaracs, no more gorilla men. Everyone was prosperous and equal. Social researchers, market analysts, government commissions, brought forth revised editions of their studies, and announced that all American society was middle class, or upper middle class, or lower middle class, or upper-upper middle class, but still middle class. No workers of any kind. This theory held sway for more than a decade.

During the Kennedy days, serious discussions about the "professionalization" of the blue collar workers were conducted in union circles. A job as a hand in a steel mill or auto plant would become a "career" similar to an accountant, a chemist, or a bank officer. They would be paid a yearly salary. No short work weeks. No lay-offs. No punching of time clocks. Just like the middle class. There would be sick leaves, sabbaticals, stock options, profit sharing. No place left for Joe Magarac!

But, by the time the blue collar workers became aware of their new status as middle class Americans, *Cybernetics* moved in, with a sworn oath to wipe out the blue collar worker with automation and computers. "In twenty years, other things being equal, most of the routine blue collar and white collar tasks that can be done by cybernation, will be," declared the 1962 report to the *Center for the Study of Democratic Institutions*. The report expressed regret that cybernetics could offer little for the future of the blue collar worker "whose innate intelligence or training is not of the highest," and proposed that they might be shipped to the less developed countries in Asia, Africa and South America!

The report forecasted: "If people cost more than machines —either in money or because of the managerial effort involved—there will be growing incentive to replace them in one way or another . . . It is possible, of course, that eventually people will not cost more than machines, because there may be so many of them competing for jobs, including a growing number of working women . . . " (Joe Magarac, where are you?)

There's no denying that technology is replacing blue collar workers in almost every industry in the United States, but the promise that they would be totally eliminated by 1980 is an unworldly pipe-dream. More than two-thirds of the cyberneticist's time-table has already expired, and the blue collar worker, excepting for the lay-offs created by recessions, is still humping it in coal mines, steel mills, auto plants, textile, construction, transportation, and in plants assembling computers. The demise of the blue collar worker has been highly exaggerated.

But the dream of blue collar workers being rooted up like weeds in a prairie recurred nightly. It was just too good a thing to let go. It was a fantastically fitting response to the muddled theorists of class versus class. It would clip the wings of the labor bosses. It would strengthen the market. It would rid the neighborhood of undesirables. A whole world of new combinations would unfold.

Census tracts, university studies, employment statistics, and sundry learned papers were presented in magical abundance to legitimize the death certificate of the blue collar worker. Even some avowed socialist scholars toyed with this painless solution to capitalism.

The United States Census showed that, beginning with 1950, the white collar and service workers were well on the way to outnumbering the blue collar workers in the United States. If you can't believe the U.S. Census, what's left? It's one agency that should be beyond suspicion. It takes some kind of nut to question their figures.

(Recently, Mrs. Mary Grady, a Chicago regional census official, when confronted by community groups, acknowledged that the 1970 census missed counting an estimated 7.7 per cent of the nation's Blacks, and even a larger percentage of the Latino population were missing. "The Bureau of the Census is taking a number of measures to combat the undercount," Mrs. Grady said. Only a nut would ask: what measures?)

(That same week, the Polish American Congress demanded that the Director of the Census Bureau give a fair count of Polish-Americans and other eastern European ethnic groups in the U.S. In the Chicago metropolitan area the census counts only 284,289 of "Polish foreign stock." The Polish American Congress' voter registration lists show 1.2 million Poles in the area! What measures will the census take to find the lost million Poles?)

How did the Census Bureau in 1950 come up with its startling discovery of the declining numbers of blue collar workers? It was an extremely complicated process. It's shameful that so much space must be allotted to baring a simple government agency with no responsibility except to count straight. But it's a serious matter when a million Poles or seven-point-seven percent of the Blacks are obliterated. And what it has attempted to do to the blue collar workers can be compared to the mass evacuation and detention of suspected national minorities during wartime (like the Japanese on the west coast). The Census records show blue collar workers as thirty-six per cent of the workforce, and white collar workers as eighteen per cent for the year 1900. And it reports that in 1950 the blue collar workers were thirty-nine per cent, while the white collar workers forged ahead to become thirty-seven per cent of the workforce, or that the blue collar population remained fixed while the white collar workers doubled their numbers.

There's an ancient axiom: there are lies, damn lies, and statistics. To this should be added, *and census figures!*

The thirty-nine per cent blue collar and thirty-seven per cent white collar figures are lies, damn lies. The original 1900 and 1950 census reports never classified one single white collar worker. This is a comparatively new census classification which began *after* the 1950 census, and it required a great deal of retroactive adjustment and guesswork to furbish up the old census reports. It was a clumsy, smeary, unbelievably infantile configuration of the workforce, which becomes apparent when the census reports *after* 1950 are examined.

In these later, post-1950 census reports the white collar and service workers were separated from the blue collar workers at the time the census was taken, but they were overwhelmingly weighted and padded to make the numbers of white collar workers greater, and blue collar workers fewer.

Only employees in the categories of manufacturing, mining, construction and transportation were considered blue collar workers. All others (except agricultural, which is a separate category) were listed as white collar and service employees. In this manner, millions of workers which common sense tells us are blue collar workers are pushed, shoved or stuffed into the white collar and service filing cabinet, so that, by the 1970 census reading, white collar and service workers are declared the majority with forty-eight per cent of the workforce, to only thirty-eight per cent of blue. A lead that's devastating.

The census bureau isn't content with listing only clerks, and salespeople, and laboratory technicians, and school teachers, and social workers, and personnel managers and the like as white collar and service workers. According to the census the white collar workers are also television repairmen, gas station attendants, auto mechanics, bus drivers (but not railroad engineers!), hotel and culinary workers (dishwashers as well as the bunnies), hospital workers (janitors as well as therapists). Absolutely no government employment is considered as blue collar, and that includes the machinist at Cape Canaveral, the printer setting up the Congressional Record, a laborer on the state highway repair crew, the electrician at a U.S. agricultural station, or a truck driver delivering the parcel post mail. They are not included in the four categories of manufacturing, mining, construction and transportation, and that's enough to change their identities.

Long before the white collar and service workers were invented as a special category of the race, there prevailed a consistent Chamber of Commerce and employer-group effort to diminish the blue collar workers, physically as well as functionally. To cut the blue collar worker down to manageable size, it must be done with precision, not aimlessly, hackingly, willy-nilly. It is necessary to cut them off from their kin, from their friends and co-workers, from their class, to reduce them, to restrict them, to isolate them. It is in that context, too, that skilled workers, the craftsmen, the master-mechanics and the higher paid workers in production like rollers in steel mills, have been designated as "aristocrats of labor," and ideologically taken out of the blue collar class and into the bourgeoise.

Labor and liberal leaders, reeling from the 1968 electoral mandate that battered their own national spokesman, stoically concluded it was an inevitable outcome of a newly-emerged social order in which the workers had become part of the middle class. The AFL-CIO *American Federationist* after the first Nixon election, carried a featured article, "The Future of the Liberal Coalition" which concluded that the coalition of workers, minorities, intellectuals, liberals and Blacks, so potent in winning national elections in the Roosevelt-Truman era, had come to an end "because the workers had merged with the bourgeoisie." After that, it wasn't hard for them to lose another election in 1972.

"If we are middle class," said AFL-CIO president George Meany at the 1972 Steelworkers Union Convention at Las Vegas, "it is because the people who started this movement many years ago decided it would be better to be middle class than low-class . . . "

Inevitably, if it no longer works, if it offers no advantages, if it hangs out bare-facedly, a lie loses its followers. Those preposterous census figures, like the Papal Bull declaring that Incas were wild animals, useful for its time, became a barrier for another time. The shrewdly mistaken doctrine of the vanishing blue collar workers, now when they're needed the most, is in the process of being revised. The great concern about the governability of democracies, has inspired the most powerful individuals in banking and industry to join with labor and liberals in the low-keyed *Trilateral Commission,* (David Rockefeller, the top executive officers of Bendix, Texas Instrument, Deere & Co., Continental Illinois Bank, Royal Dutch Petroleum, the Rothchild Financial Holdings, The Commission of the European Community, Mitishubi, SONY, Bank of Tokyo, Nmura Securities, and also I. W. Abel and Lane Kirkland of the AFL-CIO, and also Georgia Governor James E. Carter and U. S. Senator Walter F. Mondale: a total of seventy-one North Americans, and an equal number of European, and Japanese personalities who fit the description of "power-elite" if anyone ever did, with Zbigniew Brezinski as the commission director.) They meet, discuss, study, plan, report, publish and do all those things people in the seats of power are likely to do if they wish to hold on to those seats.

There's nothing anti-blue collar about the *Trilateral Commission.* Life's too short, and the world of finance and energy and proteins and markets can't afford the perverse luxury of hate. That's for the lunatic fringe. The times are getting tough, and as they now see it, the blue collar workers are to be won over as allies: the carrot, not the stick. The threat of con-

tinuing inflation and unemployment is frightening the day-
lights out of the ruling circles. The disclosures of unprecedent-
ed political and corporate corruption in the U.S., Europe and
Japan, have created serious defections. Traditional authority
of family, church, and state is losing its hold, and though it
hasn't yet happened, authority could conceivably break down
in the workplace too. The cynicism of the young, and an in-
quisitiveness about the status of workers in socialist countries,
weighs like a nightmare. People are sick with the fear of war,
and they don't seem to trust their political and military leaders. Shouldn't something be done to see that, if barricades go
up anywhere, the blue collar workers will be on the right side?

Documents are being published showing that these are the
matters the power-elite is conferring about these days, and
there are abundant signs that the blue collar worker is once
again being wooed (they can feel it in their bones) to become
a part of a new, liberal, coalition—at least for a long enough
period to win a few more elections, and perhaps help to restore
faith in the system. The U.S. Census bureau seems ready to
cooperate with a new set of statistics, and that could be helpful. And it appears that the blue collar worker in the likeness
of Joe Magarac is being readied for another cosmetic revision.
For how long a period, remains to be seen.

II A Blue Collar Hero
Is Something To Be

In view of the prevailing tendency in literature, film, theater, and the public media, to present modish stereotypes of the blue collar worker, the reader here is forewarned that uncovering *the* typical blue collar worker is an academic pipe-dream, an expedient for shifty cultists, or an unconscious yielding to class snobbishness.

The blue collar workers are as complex as any other grouping in society. However, like the university, the military, the market place, the stock exchange, the monastery, or wherever people, after sleep, spend the most hours of their lives, the workplace has its own distinctive flavor and quality, and, though it clearly stamps the blue collar worker with many markings and impressions, it does not uniformly shape the blue collar worker into a single, predictable, character.

The vignettes that follow are intended to illustrate the distinctive and overriding influence of the workplace in the lives of the blue collar worker, in the very broad sense suggested by Abraham Lincoln's message to Congress that, "The strongest bond of human sympathy, outside the family relationship, is one uniting all working people, of all nations, and tongues and kindreds," or by the Yakut proverb that says, "The first smith, the first shaman, and the first potter were blood brothers," or by Karl Marx's "Workers of the world, unite and fight. You have nothing to lose but your chains and a world to win."

Chapter Three

Taking Sides

He had never been to sea, but for as far back as he could remember everyone called him *Sailor.* On the suggestion of the midwife who delivered him he was given the name *Xavier,* for the Jesuit missionary credited with many miracles and the conversion of many converts. But no kid in Hegewisch could survive with such a tearful name, which was why he was called *Sailor,* even by his father.

Sailor's father, Jakey, landed at the port of Boston, Massachusetts, in 1912 or '13, after a long and stormy voyage from his native land of Poland. He was quickly "processed" by immigration authorities, and was presented to an "agent" who spoke his native tongue and who walked him, and a dozen or so others who had sailed with him, to a waiting bus. They rode half way across the country, and debussed at Hegewisch, a small settlement on the far south of the city of Chicago, Illinois. It was a quiet and well-kept Germanic community of frame homes and stores which had survived the Great Fire, and was then becoming a "changing community" with new Polish families employed by the steel mills moving in. Someone, another "agent", had arranged a boarding house for Jakey, and the very next day, before he had a chance to try walking on land again, he was delivered to Republic Steel, ready to go to work at his new job as laborer in the Yard Department.

Jakey fitted in well at the mill. He was strong, steady, cheerful. He was lonely. The "boarding-house lady" had a sister, still in Poland, who would make a good wife for Jakey. She immigrated to Hegewisch, and, after he saved enough money to set up house, they were married. Sailor was their first-born. Three more followed in rapid succession by the time Sailor was six.

Sailor went to school, where the Sisters spoke and taught in Polish. English was a second language. At home there were few words in any language spoken. There was a gentle quietness, except for the children's patter. It was a family not disposed to conferences or arguments or plans, and Sailor was embarrased and edgy with the contrast at school, where everyone was called upon to recite, and to perform. He was frightened in the classroom, and, despite the Sisters' frequent scoldings and wallops on his innocent head, learning to read or spell in any language seemed hopeless. Not that he felt incapable. It seemed to Sailor that the Sister was more pleased when he failed. These were mysteries to be unravelled only by the chosen ones.

At home it was different. He got things done. He helped out doing odd jobs available to strong boys in Hegewisch. The money he earned helped to pay the rent, buy coal, and provide more food for the family. The twenties—the roaring twenties —aren't plesant for Sailor to reminisce about. For blue collar workers living in the cellar of society, the 1920's have very little resemblance to the romantic world of the *Great Gatsby*. The celebrities of the world hardly affected the lives spent almost exclusively in getting those things like food, clothing, the rent money, heat in the winter, payment for the doctor.

Sailor's childhood ended early. If he had a lust for adventure, he was compelled to abandon it. Playtime was taken up with work, and being a father to his younger brother.

The Great Depression, of course, brought more distress to Sailor's house. Though his father worked two or three days a week in the mill, the pay was low, and there were now six mouths to feed. The extra money Sailor earned helped add a few more pieces of pork to the daily fare of gravy and bread, but it wasn't enough. He wanted a full-time job.

It was the winter of 1936, Sailor was sixteen years old, running with a gang that was in frequent scrapes. Small stuff, petty stuff, nobody had much worth ripping off in Hegewisch during the Great Depression. Sailor, inevitably, was arrested. Caught stealing a sackfull of coal off the railroad car—a common blue collar crime in the thirties. He went before a Chicago judge, beneath whose black judicial robes there beat a compassionate heart, and he pronounced a merciful and practical sentence. One year in jail, suspended, with the provision that Sailor get a job. And the judge suggested Republic Steel, where work was beginning to pick up.

Thankful for his lucky break, Sailor carried a letter from the judge, and was immediately hired as a laborer in the twelve inch mill at Republic Steel. It was a finishing mill, producing small rods and bars, employing the most antiquated techniques of the time. Sailor's job was to clean up scrap and scale from the mill and having it hauled away by a crane. His rate of pay was 46½ cents an hour, but he could earn more if and when he would fill in on a higher rated job from which the regular employee had reported off, and when and if he were to work overtime.

With the invasion of the German armies into Poland, steel came into great demand, and the twelve inch mill was breaking records producing war material. The CIO was beginning to organize the workers in the industry. The United States Steel Corporation dramatically signed a union contract covering its production and maintenance workers throughout the entire corporation. (It was rumored to be a secret deal involving the White House, to win over the steelworkers for war against the Germans).

Sailor heard some talk around, about a union at Republic—about a $5 a day minimun wage, about a signed contract and other highly charged phrases. While changing his clothes in the washroom one day, a Swedish crane operator (in the 30s only Swedes were permitted on cranes—no "Hunkies" or "Dagoes" or "Polacks") approached Sailor and quietly asked him to sign a card to join the Steelworkers Organizing Committee (SWOC), the forerunner of the United Steelworkers of America. Sailor shook his head. He didn't know about a union; wasn't sure he wanted to join; he would talk to his father about it. It all sounded so confusing, and he thought, "Why didn't some of my Hegewisch friends mention the union to me? Why this guy I don't even know, and who gives me a hard time when I ask him for a 'lift'?"

Somehow, Sailor sensed the union could get him into trouble. He didn't talk to his father. He didn't talk to anyone.

The next day the crane operator said, "Hey, you better sign a card and join the CIO. You know, the plant's gonna be on strike." And again Sailor told him he had to think it over. After that nobody bothered him.

And then, on May 26, 1937, a strike was called at the plant, to begin with the change of shift at 11 P.M. The union announced the strike was called because the company refused to recognize the union and sign a contract. By 9 P.M. a picket line had formed across the street from the Republic plant at 116th and Burley Avenue.

Spokesmen for the steel company, in a letter addressed to its employees, signed by Tom Girdler (immortalized by his vow to go back to the farm "and pick apples before I would recognize a union") said, in the letter, "it (the union) is attempting to prevent free American citizens from earning a living at jobs they want to pursue," and asked, in bold type, "must Republic and its men submit to communistic dictates and terrorism of the CIO?"

The picketing was joined by workers from several other plants in the South Chicago and Indiana area where unions had been established, which gave substance to the company's claims that the union was an "outside", alien, imported organization, and that Republic workers were being used for some sinister cause.

The label of "outsiders" in such an unfamiliar and volatile situation, while unrelated to the basic issue, was a powerful repellant to those who were confused and undecided. The idea of being blocked from going to work by people who have no authority and don't come from the same community or same plant could indeed be frightening. People who own little or nothing always fear invasion from "outsiders". Outsiders? To some, depending on how restricted their life has been, "outsiders" come from another country, another state or county, another city, another social class, another industry, another plant, even another department within a plant! They can be spotted on sight! Blue collar workers, who have been excluded from participating in most of the decisions that control their lives, react, none the less, with mistrust towards advice from "outsiders".

Sailor worked days, and hadn't seen the picketing on the night shift. The following morning, as the blood-orange sun rose out of Lake Michigan, as if it was washed up by a giant wave, Sailor walked, as usual, the two-mile path to the plant, half aware that foot traffic that morning was sparser than the day before. At the plant gate there was a CIO sound truck and a large group of picketing workers. There was excitement, shouting, jostling and cries of "Scab!" City police were shoving, shouting and roughing up the picketers.

Sailor hadn't yet fully decided in his mind about the CIO and unions. There were some matters he would like to have cleared up: where does the union come from? is the union breaking the law? could he be fired for joining? how will he live if he doesn't work? will the Swedes and Irish and Germans still be the bosses in the plant? But it was now too late to ask questions. The foreman had told him the day before that if he joined the strikers and stayed off of work, he would be violating his parole, and why should he get mixed up with a bunch of communists.

Choking with his own breath, his eyes fixed on the blacktop roadway, seeing or speaking to nobody, Sailor followed a group of workers who walked by the picketline into the plant.

That day, after changing into his work clothes, he told his foreman he felt sick, and thought he should go back home. He had a tightness and rawness in his chest, as though he were inhaling hot steel crystals with every breath. The foreman told him to sit down near the outside door and take it easy. When he felt better he could start work. The mill was "down" (not operating) for stand changes, and Sailor wasn't missed. When the mill "blew up" (signal to begin rolling), the foreman told Sailor the mill was short one "catcher", and when he felt better he could fill the job for the rest of the turn. Sailor's eyes widened. He took his first deep breath that day. It was like a rebirth. That part of him that was cold and dead suddenly thawed back into life. The job of "catcher" had been his nightly recurring dream. It was what he had his eye on from the first day he came to the twelve inch mill.

Sailor said he was ready to go to work. Ready to break in on his new job as "catcher". (With long iron tongs in both hands, you snatch the long thin rod of cherry-red steel travelling along rotating rolls, and you whip the rod with a well-controlled jerk, to deliver it to another bed of rolls. The rod travels through a mill stand that reduces its diameter and increases its length, and as the rod grows thinner and longer, you whip it again towards another mill stand that further reduces its diameter. Then it is sheared into uniform lengths.)

("Catchers" are known for their nimble control of heat and momentum. They grasp the hot steel bars snaking down the rolls with the ease and balance of an Olympic gymnast, aware that a single false move, one wasted motion, one lapse of attention, could mean disaster).

(The "catcher" has been replaced in most steel mills by machinery that performs the job electrically).

Sailor worked four hours overtime that day, to make up for the time he was recuperating at the open door. When, at that irregular quitting time, he left the plant, there were no pickets, and Sailor hoped that there was some kind of treaty of peace . . . .

That night 200 city police officers, led by Captains John Prendergast and James Mooney, sailed into the union picket line and arrested 40 men.

The next morning, approaching the plant entrance, Sailor saw a number of pickets. He didn't know any of them. There were none from the twelve inch mill. He wasn't sure about the rest of the plant, but there was no strike in his department. Everybody, or most everybody, was working. Would he fill in again today as the catcher? Soon he might become the regular catcher. He would buy an automobile. Perhaps get married. Or, perhaps he should turn back and go home. Could his entire future depend on this single day, this single decision? As he paused, the mill foreman, driving by, shouted, "Hey, Sailor, I'll drive you into the plant. Get in." The decision was made for him.

In the locker room, the workers were notified of a meeting of the twelve inch mill employees to be held that morning in the millwright shop. "A safety meeting," the foreman laughed.

Several management officials were at the meeting, including Frank Lauerman and J. L. Hyland. They spoke briefly, praising the men for their loyalty. They said only a handful of "troublemakers" were out on strike. Then one of the foremen made a talk that came to the point. He was no public speaker, but his message came through: there were men on the outside —"outsiders"—who were armed, and were planning to break into the plant to destroy the machinery and beat up the employees. Then he turned his head to a corner of the shop where several bundles of long wooden sledge-hammer handles were piled, and said "we have a right to protect ourselves." Then he announced that everyone would sleep inside the plant that night, because pickets might try to stop anyone from coming back again. There were cots, and drinks, and there would be hot meals.

(Later reports from the United States Senate Committee, headed by Wisconsin's Senator LaFollette, disclosed that the corporation had purchased guns, clubs, grenades and other weapons. Eighty five Chicago policemen were permanently quartered inside the plant. The Republic Steel Corporation had spent $1,900,000 to break the strike, which was one-fourth of the corporation's profit for the year).

Sleeping inside the plant. It didn't sit well with most of the men. It was like being prisoners. Crossing the picket line is one thing; sleeping in the plant something quite different. To wake up in the hot mill and go right back to work, with nothing in between, would be too much. If pickets were going to invade the plant, being asleep would be the worst possible position.

Men, quiet, uninvolved, intimidated men, who seldom in their lives had ventured a social or political opinion, were now stung by a political decision already made for them, and from which it was too late to appeal. Whom do you see, where do you go, is there a telephone number to call, to tell somebody in authority that you've decided to go home? And how many days and nights will you be required to nest inside the plant? Nobody seemed to have any answer.

At that moment Sailor felt transported into another world. And again he felt that same rawness in his chest he had when he first crossed the picket line. This was his only experience with unions and strikes, but the way it looked to him now, with clubs being passed around, sleeping inside the plant, serving whiskey and food, it was like joining some secret order. All that was missing was raising your hand and repeating the oath. What had been, in his mind, a very personal matter to be accounted for to nobody but himself, had become transformed, somehow, to a solemn commitment to a faith and a cause he knew very little about.

The next day was Memorial Day, and the CIO called a labor rally and picnic at "Sam's Place," a friendly restaurant and tavern near Republic Steel. The union strike headquarters were there, too. There was a big turn-out, joined by the strikers and their wives and children, workers from other plants, steelworkers from the "Big Mill" of U.S. Steel where the union had a signed contract, also students and professors from the University of Chicago (investigated twenty years later, by the Illinois State Legislature for "communist influence"), artists, writers, social workers, revolutionists, and curious citizens from many walks of life. It was regarded by many as a day to bear witness, a day of commitment, a day of prayer, a plea and a rebuttal to those powerful business interests who were trying to block the social revolution promised by Franklin Delano Roosevelt.

National CIO leaders Leo Kryszky, Nick Fontaccio, Joe Weber, George Patterson—first generation Americans— spoke to the rally zealously defending the patriotic ideals of America's most solemn anniversary, which had to be preserved in Labor's rights to a union. Then they decided to have a parade to the gate of the mill.

It wasn't really a parade. There was no rolling of drums or flourish of trumpets. No candidates for elections waving to the crowds. No decorated automobiles with beauty queens and celebrated stars advertising "Sam's Place—A Good Place to Eat." Only workers and their supporters, holding quickly-drawn signs proclaiming labor's rights, lined up loosely and without symmetry, strolling and singing in the warm afternoon sun.

It appeared that the Chicago city police were convinced, too, that this was no Memorial Day parade, that, as the steel corporation's president had warned so many times, it was a revolutionary mob bent on wrecking the Republic plant, murdering the loyal workers, and setting up the dictatorship of the proletariat.

In a matter of minutes the prairie resembled a scene viewed

on television during the Viet Nam war some thirty years later, except that the dead and wounded weren't Vietnamese. They were Polish, Hungarian, Serbian, Croatian, Italian, Blacks, Mexicans, Swedish—blue collar workers, and innocent children screaming with horror and pain. Films of these events, unlike battles in the Viet Nam war, were confiscated and suppressed for many years, as unfit for public viewing.

The killing of ten workers and the wounding of almost one hundred others in that Memorial Day parade was a fair measure of the social climate in 1937. Whether there would be more public sympathy for such victims today than there was in 1937, or whether the massacre of workers in Chicago conditioned Americans to accept the Nazi atrocities in Europe, or the atrocities of Americans in Viet Nam, or Kent State college, or in uncounted Black ghettos, is indeed disturbing to speculate. "Wounded prisoners of war might have expected and received better treatment," reported the U.S. Senator La-Follette's Investigating Committee.

In the twelve inch mill, among the interned employees, the talk of the killings and the strike was strangely uneasy and spare. They were cut off from the world and knew only what they read in the newspapers that were spirited into the plant. They discovered that one of the workers killed was a twelve inch mill worker's younger brother who came to the parade from one of the Indiana mills. A collection in the mill for flowers and a cash donation to the family was started. It totaled four hundred dollars, the equivalent of a half year's pay at that time. It was the biggest collection for a deceased relative anyone could remember.

Out of respect for the brother, Sailor felt he should go to the wake. It was uncomfortable for him, because he didn't know the family. But he made up his mind to view the body, say a prayer, and leave. Before he got to the casket, a teenage, college-type girl, with a big CIO button pinned to her sweater, stopped him, looked directly into his eyes, and shouted, "You murdered him, you lousy, rotten scab!"

(In the experience of the Åmerican worker, there is no more explosive a subject than *scabbing,* and the term *scab* is unique in our language. Different from other expletives, calling someone a *scab* is never subject to misinterpretation. It is direct and inflexible. It can't be mellowed or softened by tone of voice or circumstances. It can't be rescinded or pardoned. Different, say, than *sonofabitch,* the most familiar title of censure or impeachment. But that word gives absolutely no clue to the actual misdeeds or depravities committed, and can be construed in a hundred different ways. It has no lasting ingredients to make it stick. Today's *sonofabitch* may be tomorrow's drinking partner, business partner or bed partner.

(Good friends may and do call each other *motherfucker* without any trace of anger or intention to insult. It's just a word. It could show opposition to language repression, or it could express unity with the ghetto, or anything and nothing.

(When the Industrial Workers of the World (I.W.W.) flourished in some parts of the country, Wobblies would greet each other with, "Hey! you ol' pigfucker!" as an expression of comradeship and affection.

(The language of the steel mills—and coal mines, and auto plants, and most workplaces—overflows with the most colorful sexual and scatalogical expletives, used as nouns, adjectives, adverbs, conjunctions, and in ways grammarians have not yet discerned, and it has been given official recognition as "mill language" by labor arbitrators deciding against a steelworker who claimed *verbal assault* by a supervisor.

(But definitely not included in this "mill language" is the word *scab.*

(Trade unions which haven't engaged in a strike for decades, are, somehow driven to reprint in their journals, some as often as once or twice a year, the classic definition of scab attributed to the famous American writer, Jack London: "After God finished the rattlesnake, the toad and the vampire, He had some awful substance with which He made the scab. A scab is a two-legged animal with a corkscrew soul, a waterlogged brain, and a combination backbone of jelly and glue. Where others have hearts, he carries a tumor of rotten principles. No man has a right to scab as long as there is a pool of water to drown his carcass, or a rope long enough to hang his body. Judas Iscariot was a gentleman compared with a scab. The modern strikebreaker is a traitor to his God, his country, his family, his class, and most of all to himself."

(In a rough scale of descent in the world of the blue collar worker, a *scab* is someone who: 1. hires on to a job in a plant where a strike is in progress, 2. continues to work in a plant where the union has declared a strike, 3. crosses a union picket line, 4. races with other worker for greater production on the job.)

Sailor, at the age of eighteen, had never heard much about *scabs*. He had knowledge of stoolies, squealers, pimps and other low characters. Hegewisch had its share of them. But it was at Republic Steel, in the strike of 1937, that he first had to deal with this American institution.

In Hegewisch, especially among the newer residents immigrated from villages of eastern Europe, families weren't torn apart by the steel strike, as was the case in the 1934 Kohler strike in Wisconsin, or the coal strikes of southern Illinois, West Virginia and Pennsylvania, or other tightly-knit communities of several generations of workers' families, where the issue of scabbing was highly personal and where labor solidarity was almost synonymous with family loyalty.

Even among employers, the issue of scabs often left deep scars. In the Homestead, Pennsylvania steel strike of 1892, the "kindly" Andrew Carnegie opposed hiring scabs to take the place of strikers in his mills, while his partner, the "ruthless" Henry Clay Frick, went ahead and recruited scabs as strikebreakers. This created a rift between the two partners, and, according to the historian, Leon Wolff, when, years later, Carnegie put out feelers through mutual friends for a burying of the hatchet, Frick sent back word to "tell your friend Carnegie that I will see him in Hell, where we are both going."

Though Sailor had never lived in Poland, his home in Hege-wisch was only a short distance from his father's birthplace in the feudal village of Kolno, where you learn early in life to obey *Authority*— the priest, the Sister, the policeman, the soldier, the boss, the landlord, whoever is in charge.

Did the union have authority in 1937? How could the union tell someone to stay off from work, when the boss said WORK? That's crazy. The boss is boss, not the union. The boss makes out the work schedule, sends you home, promotes you when the time comes, pays you, not the union. It hardly made sense to Sailor.

It is said that it requires several generations to train certain highly skilled artisans, like coppersmiths, jewel-setters, print-makers, glass-blowers, wine-makers, and many others that have been lost to civilization. How many generations does it require to produce "class-consciousness?" Can one acquire it from breathing in the smoke and gas of the coke ovens, from incessant hellish noises of iron against iron, from the hurts and bruises of aching hands and muscles? How long must one work in a steel mill to get all that inside the blood and guts and the mind?

It seems well established in the study of humanities that lasting and successful movements in society must be rooted in history, legend, rituals, songs, heroes, saints, martyrs, rene-gades. The Labor Movement in the United States hasn't had an easy time forming such foundations with the workers, due, in part, to the stubborn opposition from employers and gov-ernment. But the labor movement itself has strangely default-ed. Never sure of its own philosophy or goals, uneasy about the mind and spirit of the workers, fearful of power, and at-tracted to the smoother road of accomodation to industry and the State, the leadership of the labor movement exerted little energy to capitalize on such events as Haymarket, Pullman, the unemployed movement, the Memorial Day Massacre. Even the memories of such established figures as Samuel Gompers, John L. Lewis, Philip Murray, are hardly noted within the trade union movement. No one has ever suggested a national holiday in their names. Unlike Blacks, who succeeded in establishing Dr. Martin Luther King's anniversary as a holiday in many states and in many union contracts, Labor has not moved to create a similar recognition for a single one of its own martyrs.

But, so far, no one has been successful in diluting or transforming the *scab* in the United States. No one has seriously attempted to martyrize the scab, in the manner of *Horst Wessel* in Nazi Germany. This is probably the only labor tradition that remains solidly in possession of the blue collar workers.

Two weeks after the Memorial Day Massacre, the union at Republic Steel backed off. The strike was terminated. It took four years more for the company to sign a contract with the union.

Sailor joined the union when it had a contract. In his own mind he was now a union man. He paid his dues monthly. Later his dues was checked off by the company, like taxes and insurance. He never had time to go to any of their meetings. Hardly any members attended, except if something important, like a contract or another strike was in the air.

When, in 1957 he was out on strike for seventeen weeks, he decided on a change. Besides, the twelve inch mill was being shut down permanently. A new, more modern, high speed fourteen inch mill was being built to take its place, and Sailor's job had been eliminated. "Catchers" were not needed in the new mill. Electronically controlled manipulators had moved in on the job. Sailor, under the terms of the union contract, was entitled to a transfer to another department, but the company didn't give him any definite answers. It never does on such matters. Finally, the company, without making a commitment, inquired if he would be interested in a foreman's job. But Sailor turned it down.

He got a job at the Ford plant in Hegewisch. The loss of fifteen years seniority wasn't easy to take. It seemed unfair.

But the deepest tragedy to Sailor was his utter failure to understand how he became such a helpless victim of the system he admired so much, how his world which held so many promises of pleasure, just when he was ready to receive them, collapsed.

Chapter Four

A Right Arm for the Company

There were large crowds of striking steelworkers and their families, on Memorial Day, 1937, scrambling through the grassy prairie which borders on the Republic Steel plant on Chicago's far south side, and, in the turbulence of the shootings, and yelling, and scuffling, young Steve's cry was barely heard. "Pa, Pa, I'm shot." And he held his left foot in both hands, staring at the flow of blood.

Just turned eleven, Steve Yuratovac was pretty young to be shot. It might have been overlooked in Lebanon, Cyprus, Vietnam, or the South African bush, but for an American, even the son of a blue collar worker, eleven was, or should have been, too young for shooting.

An eye-witness, Dr. Lawrence Jacques, who attended Steve and others caught in the cross-fire of bullets on that Memorial Day, reported to a federal committee hearing conducted by Wisconsin's Senator LaFollette:

" . . . It sounded like machine-gun fire. Within five minutes there were approximately thirty or forty people bleeding, groaning, screaming, and dying . . . Among the wounded were two children, a fifteen year old girl, and *an eleven year old boy.*"

The eleven year old boy—that was Steve. A hot pellet hit him in the foot and tore off a piece of the heel, as if it were part of a rabbit or wild bird. He was at once in pain, and intensely aware he needed help. "Pa, Pa, I'm shot," he cried again.

His father was a striker, and Steve trustingly went along with him to attend the picnic and rally at Sam's Place, near the plant. His sister, cousin, and "Gypsy", a local strike leader who lived next door, all went together, and nobody had the faintest suspicion there would be any shooting.

Young Steve could have spent the holiday in a number of more boyishly suitable ways, but he wished to please his father, who wished to please "Gypsy". "Gypsy" had settled opinions on raising children. "If you want your boy to grow up a man, take him with you wherever you go," he would freely counsel his fellow-strikers.

The wounded strikers were loaded into police vans like cord-wood and delivered to whatever hospitals would accept them. But Steve's father, on the advice of "Gypsy", gathered his wounded son in his own loving arms, and carried him home, cursing in the choicest Serbian all along the way, threatening merciless reprisals for the blood-letting.

Steve had his father's assurance he hadn't been killed, and he rather enjoyed the sensation of having leaped into manhood, a union brother, singled out by those "Gypsy" unvaryingly referred to as "the bosses." When, on arriving home, his mother let out a cry of pity, Steve forced a smile and asked, "Ma, were you shot too?"

He didn't know until many years later that his heel-wound, not as far-famed as Achilles', had been, nonetheless, accorded respectable literary notice in *Citizens,* Levin's novel of the "little steel" strike.

The Slavic section of the far southeast Chicago, where Steve grew up, was, in appearance and style, little different from the other numerous ethnic settlements in close proximity to the steel mills. It was an enclave within a community of a big city, with its own stores, school, precinct captain, priest, peddlers, bakery, tavern, policeman. In this respect, Serbian, Polish, Greek, Italian, Croatian, Hungarian and other ethnic workers' settlements seem to have been poured from the same mold. Indeed, they had more flavor of *class* than *ethnicity*. It was in later years, that *ethnicity* was calculatingly heightened out of all proportion. The Serbo-Croatian enclave was a few hundred yards from Republic Steel, and also close to U.S. Steel, Youngstown Sheet and Tube, Interlake Iron, Valley Mold, and Wisconsin Steel. It was made up of ageing two and three-flat buildings that needed ceaseless repair to rescue them from the corrosive emissions of the mills. Discoloration, rotting, cracking, disjointing—whatever could afflict a building in such a setting—was certain to befall this community. And for a people who had until then pursued peaceful agrarian occupations in the Hercogovinian hills, it took some time to get accustomed to the hellish clatter of switching freight trains, and the continual pounding, and roaring, and shrieking of the mills.

But in America, noise, like smoke, meant work, jobs, meat on the table, shoes for the kids, coal in the bin. Ecologists were a kind of incoherent and powerless clique of the Audubon Societies and the Izaak Walton Leagues. Franklin D. Roosevelt, seeking votes in Chicago during the Great Depression, pledged that "smoke would come out of the stacks again." Those were the *smokeless thirties*.

(It has become a fetish of historiographers of the twentieth century to dub each decade with a cool and all-embracing identity—the *roaring* twenties, the *beat* forties, the *silent* fifties, the *insurgent* sixties, the *decadent* seventies—with the general understanding that each prefix articulates a new life style, a new social consciousness, a new political destiny. In that context, it is the life styles, the activism and the ideologies of the avant-garde writers, artists and musicians, students, editors of underground journals, fashion designers, film directors and others whose vision of what is and what can be in our society is free-handed and flighty, that give the decade its description. The blue collar workers are systematically shut out of their historical judgements. None of their nimbly-named decades of the twentieth century gives any clue to the basic lives of the fifty million workers who punch a time-clock, for whom the mode of life has changed so little from decade to decade, persistently pressed with mundane problems of unemployment, wage rates, speed-up in the work-place, overtime, industrial safety, class, racial, ethnic and sexual discrimination.)

This seeming diversion from our account of Steve is in the way of getting to the bottom of his prophetic attraction to the steel mills, and the climactic surrender of his right arm to the company.

With the sole breadwinner out on a prolonged strike, how Steve's family was able to survive is an experience as complex as that period itself. In other times, striking workers would get help from friends or family members who weren't on strike. But in the '30s, strikers' contacts with employed people were rare. Steve's recollection that he "never went hungry" during the strike or depression must be taken with a pinch of salt. (It's strange how many children of the Great Depression swear they never went hungry, especially those who have since risen into a higher economic circle of society, and resent the newer crop of welfare recipients.) He boasted of the in-bred strength of his family to weather the storm. They wouldn't properly fit into the sociologists' definition of "the culture of poverty." Their community wasn't a slum. It was a tightly-knit Serbo-Croatian workers' community, and, like other ethnic communities, the inhabitants were drawn narrowly together by a common language, religion and culture. Though varying slightly in the degree of their poverty, it would be most difficult to distinguish class differences. They accepted their status without reservation, with no thoughts of shifting to some other more elevated, less impoverished unit. The affluence they knew about was of another race, another community, another society into which they never dreamed of intruding—of owners and bosses—as far out of their reach as the family of King Peter.

Every family, it seemed, had something unusual and mysterious that helped them survive, some fractional economic privilege, some ambiguous windfall of farm produce, some gifts or thefts, some lucky find. There's no other way to account for the survival of those without income from their labor or sale of goods.

A unique ingredient of Steve's family life—the fierce involvement in the activities of the union—made a difference, too, not materially, but psychologically. The excitement of picketing and union meetings and workers congregating in his home, made it easier to accept the monotony of the simple table, the dark looks of the landlord, and other discomforts.

They also kept two goats, a capital accumulation from better days, that grazed off the company-owned prairie grass, in criminal violation of the city code, and produced rich milk and delicious fata cheeses. Together with the flat pans of unleavened Serbian bread which his mother baked daily, this was the mainstay of their diet. (There is no attempt to explain how the flour for the bread was scraped up.)

It wasn't until around 1939, when the New Deal was about winding up, that Steve's father was declared eligible for a WPA job, and he worked for several months raking leaves in Calumet Park, earning $50 a month in cash, to pay rent and other urgent items. In 1942 he got back to work in the mill, and getting a paycheck every week was like a resurrection, or as Steve put it, "with the eagle shittin' regular, we thought we were rich." Later, Steve's oldest sister got a job in the local bakery, and by the standards of the community, they were definitely out of the depression, and Steve, a high school student, was being urged by the family to study hard and become an engineer. In a family where nobody had ever finished high school, how Steve would become an engineer wasn't very clearly pictured.

At Bowen High School, in South Chicago, Steve spent a great deal of time dreaming about his cousin in the Navy, about his dark-eyed English teacher who had "fantastic" legs, about his future as an engineer, or maybe as a driver in the Indianapolis 500 mile Speedway. (In that intensely ethnic community, Vukovich the racing star, was a hero, greater than any other sports figure.) Like any full-grown sixteen year oldster, he was ready to plunge into the adult world.

Bowen High was a nasty place in the 1940s. Nothing like what was portrayed in *Graffiti* and other movies of that decade. It was more like a correctional institution, where the chief concerns of the keepers were attendance, noise, clear hallways, lunchroom order, after school rumbles, "cuts". The girls and boys—greasers by definition— reacted like normal inmates, some learning to conform, some waiting to be sprung, and others, like Steve, ambivalent about the entire matter. If he was going to be an engineer, he would have to shape up, compromise, take all the "crap" they handed out; and if he wanted adulation at home, he'd certainly have to do better.

He began "cutting classes", leaving at noon, and going to the Loop to the movies. The Loop was sensational. The rhythm of the lunch-hour crowds pouring out of offices was like a pageant. The men appeared so full of confidence, like they had the world by the short hairs, and the women, smelling of expensive perfumery, seemed so young and dainty and easy, beside whom, the girls in South Chicago, in their cheap print dresses, and looking like they had just finished their house chores, could never measure up. It was so different. The tall buildings, banks, departments stores, restaurants, monuments, the restlessness of slowly moving traffic and the continuous whistling of the police were the substances of his thoughts and dreams. He cut his classes every day for a week, to look over the Loop, and then to a movie to see Ida Lupino (who was a dead ringer for his English teacher, with the "fantastic" legs) and Humphrey Bogart in *High Sierra*.

Bowen High soon caught up with Steve's cutting classes, and suspended him. His Ma had to go to the school principal and plead in broken English to have him reinstated. She cried from the humiliation she suffered, and that night there was no talk or laughter at the supper table. You would think someone had come down with a deadly disease. Steve didn't know how to make excuses, he didn't believe he had done anything terrible, except for the hurt to his Ma.

The next day he saw immediately what great changes had taken place at Bowen. The teachers weren't a bit friendly. They froze him out. Only his English teacher (he was certain she was trying to seduce him) was amiable. It was his class in "social studies" where it all come to a head. The teacher, O'Hara, a "sour-looking pussy" in his early thirties, became annoyed at Steve and screamed at him that he was "a dumb Hunky" and "belonged in the steel mills."

James Bryant Conant, former Harvard University president, in a book, *Slums and Suburbs*, published ten years after this incident at Bowen High, and so, of course, in no position to know about it, wrote that "the educational experience of youth should fit their subsequent employment. There should be a smooth transition from full-time schooling to a full-time job."

Steve and Conant probably wouldn't understand each other, but Steve fully understood O'Hara's remark about where "dumb Hunkies" belong, because he had heard it on many occasions. Steve got up from his seat, walked over to O'Hara, slow and easy, like he had seen Bogart do in *High Sierra,* and planted a sharp right jab on his chin, ending, abruptly and forever, Steve's schooling at Bowen High.

There was no full-time job waiting for Steve, as advocated by the Harvard president, but there was a full-time war going on, and Steve, who had for months had it on his mind and had discussed it with his Navy cousin, went to the post-office to talk to a recruiting officer, and signed up.

"It wasn't that I was so friggin' patriotic," he was careful to tell his friends, "but I'd have been drafted in a few months anyhow, and I didn't want to be shoved into some dog-face outfit. Not this Hunky." He asked for service in the Navy, and he thought they said that was fine, but somehow he landed into an infantry outfit and became a "dogface."

It's never easy to get a straight story from a foot soldier in World War II. It might be they feel their own role so trifling in the enormous global military strategy, and their own body and mind and spirit become so blurred and insignificant, that they simply don't clearly know, except for what they read, were told, or from films, but not from what they had seen with their own eyes, how they were connected to the war. Steve, if he said it once, said a hundred times, that "only guys who never had experiences as a civilian talk about their war experiences," hinting that there wasn't all that much to talk about, that war experiences weren't that individual. It's interesting that most of the war stories told in the plant had very little direct association with war or soldiering. They were about civil matters, personalities in their outfits, snafus in the mess halls or supply depots, rackets of the officers, the quality of the booze, the odors, talents and prices of the whores, run-ins with MPs and "ninety day wonders," winnings at crap games, stale barracks jokes. The blue collar workers in war were and are as removed from the essential nature and purpose of their military life as they were, and are, of their civilian life. Steve's summary of his two years in France was not irrelevant to blue collar workers' orientation, explaining, in all seriousness, that if he had his way he'd have given that country back to the Germans, who "at least kept it clean. For a civilized country, you've never seen such filthy fuckin people." The tolerance of blue collar workers for Fascism had been carefully cultivated for decades. Steve's comment that "if it weren't for the Japs, I wouldn't have ever enlisted," was accepted in the plant as a reliable diagnosis of the problem, as was also his assertion that "the real enemy was Russia, not Germany." And that "before Pearl Harbor the only people in the U.S. against Germany were the Jews."

Steve dallied for a good while after his discharge from the service, using up all the available benefits for returned veterans—mustering-out pay, unemployment pay, set-ups at the Legion bar, sociable neighborhood reunions, dates with flirtatious girls who had grown up while he was off to war, a first visit to his Pa's grave, where he wept without restraint, bitter, too, that the Red Cross hadn't notified him in time to attend the funeral, a lamb barbecue in his honor at the St. Archangel Michael Serbian Eastern Orthodox Church, numberless flat pans of Ma's homemade bread with cartons of homogenized milk (the goats were gone, declared a city nuisance). When he had his fill, and money ran out, he talked about his future with his Ma, who, though never having ventured outside her boundaries of a half dozen blocks to shop for food, go to Church, visit her daughter, see the doctor, had a mystifying insight into the broader world. She pleaded with him to "stay away from the mills."

Had it been twenty years later, Steve could have been assured by the advice of David Halberstam, in *The Best and the Brightest,* though it wasn't addressed to blue collar workers. "To make it in America, to rise, there has to be some sort of propellant; sheer talent helps, but except in very rare instances, talent is not enough. Money helps, family ties and connections help; for someone without these the way to the power elite can seem too far, too hopeless to challenge."

Steve didn't aspire to go quite that far, and by no stretch of the imagination, by no conceivable stroke of luck or magic, by no romantic act of charity, by no inherited propellant or thriving talent did he have any genuine hope that doors would open for him that were closed to his father or friends in his community. He had no offers or prospects. Nobody called him on the phone. The Trib Help Wanted ads were mostly for salesmen, and offices, and for people with education. A job in the

Loop would be nice, but, but, but . . . .

His father's pal "Gypsy" had become a "wheel" in the union, and he could supply "a propellant" to get him a job at Republic Steel. There are worse places to work. This is close to home, the pay is better than some of the small shops, you don't need any special skill. Everybody starts at the bottom, and they teach you what you need to know.

Steve was hired as a millwright helper in the blooming mill. It was five job grades above a laborer, and the opportunities for promotion were better. It was something like an apprenticeship—on-the-job training, but no trade school classes—which led to the job of first-class millwright, when a vacancy occured and the helper was qualified. (Apprenticeship in its classic form has all but disappeared in the United States, for reasons examined in a later chapter.)

The millwright helper's duties were to help the millwright in whatever he asked him to do, to follow his instructions, fetch the tools he requests, clean them up, scrap the unrepairable parts, swing the sledgehammer, hook up the burning outfit, learn how the mill operates and how to prevent a breakdown. There's a whole lot of wear and tear on blooming mill equipment when it is being pummeled every minute, every second of the day with hot, twenty-ton ingots lunging and banging against the rolls. Bearings burn out, mill-rolls freeze, hydraulic systems spring leaks, oil systems rupture, water pressure fails, shear knives crack, conveyor chains snap, manipulators break down. All part of a millwright's day.

As though his life depended on it, Steve never let the millwright out of his sight. He scrutinized every motion, and strained to every word. On the other hand, the millwright was visibly annoyed by Steve's intensive questions, accused him of bugging him, and reminded him that it took years to learn the millwright's trade, and to get off his back. Steve was convinced the millwright was prejudiced against him because he was young, and because he was Serbian, and that he was keeping him from learning anything about the job. He was kept busy chasing tools, cleaning up grease and pushing a broom, so he wouldn't be around when repairs were being made to the mill—a not-too-subtle staple of every skilled worker's survival strategy. Steve was beginning to boil, and one morning when the millwright was thumbing over a blue print, holding it purposely out of Steve's view, as though it were personal and confidential, he popped off, "Look here, Polak, I'm gonna' learn everything there is to know about this fuckin millwright job, no matter what you think. Cut this bullshit. I lost four fuckin years in the army, while you were here sittin' on your cunt, making easy money, paying off on a house, stashin' it away in the bank. There's nothing you can do this Hunky can't do. I'm not trying to take away your job, but if it was the only millwright job open, I'd fuckin well take that."

That little talk might have helped. At least the chasing around stopped, and this gave him more opportunities to observe independently. Steve and the millwright, at times, wouldn't exchange a single word for the entire eight hour turn. When there was a major breakdown, and repair crews from other shops came to assist, Steve would get a chance to pitch in, sledging, fitting, cutting, or whatever had to be done. He wasn't thought of as a competitor by the other repair crews, and they were only too happy to let him do their work while they rested or had coffee.

In large workplaces, supervision has always been ambivalent about this intimidating game of giving "a hard time" to new employees. It creates division and suspicions within the work force, which can be useful to the company in undermining unionization or any concerted employee initiative. It keeps the older workers on their toes, and more appreciative. It makes the new workers more eager to learn, more ambitious for promotion, and weeds out the weak. In many ways, it's similar to the organized aggression of the old-timers against new inmates or recruits in prisons or the military. It's a morale-builder and essential to discipline, they say. Though seemingly spontaneous, rooted in the biology of the human race, it looms out of the same pattern that pits races and ethnic groups and national minorities against one another.

When Steve's morale would be sinking to its lowest depths, and he would feel he could no longer endure the humiliation and insults that went with his job, he considered requesting a transfer to another department or quitting altogether, but then he would be rescued by a "report-off" of a millwright which would give him the opportunity to fill in as the millwright for a day or two. This restored him and helped him decide he would stick it out.

Steel to rebuild war-torn Europe and Japan was in great demand, and the mill expanded its production with additional equipment and workers. This opened up jobs for millwrights, and Steve, on the basis of his seniority and ability, became, at last, a millwright.

There are some jobs in a steel mill, as in most industries, which are considered so critical to its operation, that, over the years, holders of such jobs are regarded as sorcerers whose cunning is legendary. They are usually without formal training, uncomfortable with prints, equations or written specifications, but as sure of themselves as the tribal medicine-men. A millwright is such a job. If they can't fix it, who? The mill superintendents? the engineers? the factory representatives? the works manager? A common scene in a rolling mill is a couple dozen top management people in their business suits and luminous white hard-hats, silent and straining at the sight of a mill come to a sudden halt, while a millwright, with insolent ease, hardly concealing the artisan's contempt for vulgar patrons, pulls on a forty-eight inch open-end wrench to unloosen a gear case cover, sledges a gear-key back into place, replaces the cover, removes his tools, and waves to the roller to start up, without a moment's thought that it might fail. All the white-hats smile with relief, and march back to their command posts.

Steve finally had the job he wanted, at least for the moment. He had his own helper, his own tools, and locker to keep them. Now he had attention, responsibilities, respect, and more money (a raise of fifty eight cents an hour). At most other jobs in a steel plant there is far less involvement in the production process, the work is much more repetitious and less varied, less of an opportunity to figure things out, than with a millwright job.

After a night out with the girl he was going to marry, Steve came to work on the "A" turn (11 P.M. until 7 A.M.). He had planned to leave her off earlier, so he could go home and catch some sleep before going to the mill, but, as they say, one beer led to another, and it was so unbearable to break up early, that he didn't even have time to pick up his lunch at home. He drove directly to the plant, and let his fiance drive herself home. He prayed for an easy night. There are some nights when there isn't a single call for a millwright, and all you do is have your helper check the mill, watch the oil levels, grease when there's time, while you catch a few winks. Steve had been a millwright for more than a year, and he was always pretty lucky on night turns.

There are theories that for some people the night has some magically stimulating effect, but this theory doesn't have many followers in the workplace. Nights, for Steve, were a curse. You never get used to them. By the time you finish your seventh night, and have worked out a bit of order in your life, you are changed to the afternoon shift, and then after seven motherless "C" turns (3 P.M. until 11 P.M.) that cut you off from everything except sleep, that forbidden, magical potion that haunts you on the "A" turn, you find yourself again working the "B" turn—ah! those glorious, orderly day turns that supposedly restore you to a normal way of life. Round and round it goes. It is said that shift work messes up your sleep, your digestion, your biology, your sex life. It certainly interferes with the social life of a single guy, courting.

Steve changed into his sweated, grease-stained work-clothes, trying desperately to shake off the drowsiness that was strangling him. Coffee was ready in the millwright shop, and he laboriously washed out his stained coffee mug. Before he had a chance to pour the coffee, he was interrupted by four sharp blasts from the roller's pulpit—the signal for a millwright. Steve looked at his helper—was that *three* or *four*? The answer came quickly with four more blasts. It sounded shriller and angrier this time. And then repeated. It was *four,* all right, validated by a phone call from the mill foreman, shouting for him to "Get your ass out there on the Rust Furnace. The door won't close." Everyone shouts in a steel mill. It's partly because of the continuous, deafening clamor, partly because steel production is terribly unsympathetic to error, partly because steel mill supervision, historically, worked close to the floor of the mill instead of panelled offices, and being loud and rough and foulmouthed proved their metal.

His orders were clear enough. He grabbed a few tools from the bench, a bar, a sledge-hammer, and turned to his helper to take care of the coffee. He climbed the iron stairway leading to the ailing furnace, which nested a couple-hundred tons of semi-finished billets in a cradle of fire. The furnace door was hung up, frozen in an open position. The heat was being lost— harmful to critical steel that must maintain an even temperature. When the door is working properly it opens and closes hydraulically at the touch control of the "heater" in charge. Why it remained open and refused to fall back, was for Steve, the millwright, to analyze, to hit the right pin, to tighten the right bolt, to pour oil on the right bearing, to make it work.

He kneeled, and strained to look behind the furnace door, blistering hot and perched like a guillotine, but stubbornly and mysteriously "fucked up"—a diagnosis covering a limitless number of mechanical disorders in any workplace.

While he was kneeling and inspecting, not given a split second's warning, and for reasons that to this day have not been settled, the hot furnace door plunged down, swift and without a wasted quiver, down, and clamped his arm to the hot platform. For a moment his whole world went into an eerie spin, and sharp jabs of seering pain attacked him from every side. One who has never experienced the pain of massive burning of the flesh, unless he aspires to become, let us say, a Dante, or a biblical preacher of damnation, should never attempt to describe Steve's suffering. It was the kind of torment he feared he would undergo if he were captured during the war, but it was far worse than that. He thought, in his agony, about hypnotizing himself into a state of painless consciousness; he thought of wild animals that chewed off their own leg to free themselves from a steel-jawed trap. But he couldn't do anything. Except submit. Surrender to a superior force.

How long it took to free his arm is a matter of dispute. The company said within a few minutes; others said longer. The door had to be pried loose, and the mill crew worked furiously with four by fours to raise the door. It had to take more than a few minutes.

At the South Chicago Community Hospital, where Republic Steel delivered all its ambulance cases, the medical team, according to witnesses, moved like it had all night, busier filling out long forms than attending to Steve. The mill officials were at hand, talking to one another, discussing how the accident might have happened and which witnesses should be called to the investigation. They neglected to notify his Ma until hours later. Steve was shamelessly abandoned. Only the blistering pain remained.

The hospital medical team determined the flesh on his entire arm had been cooked too long, and amputated it all the way to the shoulder.

Steve lost a full year, recovering from his accident. He lived off workmen's compensation of $56 a week, about one half his earnings as a millwright. Under the workmen's compensation law he received a total payment of $14,000—that was the going rate for workers' arms in the *silent fifties*. (With later inflation, the law was amended and today he would receive $20,891.50 for the loss of the arm.)

(Workmen's compensation is a piece of "labor legislation" that was fought for by the liberal and labor movement to protect the workers who could never afford to go into the courts, hire lawyers, and win a suit against a powerful corporation. And to be fair to both sides, the law also protects the corporation from law suits by injured workers. What could be fairer!

(The chief counsel for the House Committee on Labor and Education, Don Baker, commented that, in some cases, "the worst thing that could happen to a family is for a man to be killed or injured on the job. They are better off economically if he quits and goes on welfare, or gets fired—or gets killed in a bar.")

For days before Steve's release by the company doctors to return to work, rumors spread that he was going "out the gate," that he was suing the company for a half million dollars, that he was going to be transferred to a desk job, that he was being "shafted," that he could never be a millwright with only one arm, that he was going to be a foreman, but nobody in authority seemed to know what Steve was going to do.

He was allowed to hang around the millwright shop for a few weeks with no duties. He just sat around, ignored by the foreman, and Steve suspected that even the other men in the shop tried to avoid him. He ate his lunch with the others, but that was about the only socializing that occured. It was as though he had some dangerously contagious disease or had a "curse" on him, that, with bad luck, could be transferred to any of them today or tomorrow.

A job as a foreman in the ten inch mill was finally offered him, and he took it. His duties there were never quite specific. He was used by the company for a variety of details, to attend hearings on accident cases, to be an expert witness in grievance hearings, to conduct tours for visitors in the plant, all kinds of one-handed lackey jobs that separated him from his friends in the mill. The men in the ten inch mill referred to him as "the one-armed bandit," but they meant no slur.

He usually responded to questions about his arm with flip one-liners—"nobody's perfect"..."women feel safer with me..." His favorite reply is what he said is an old Indian proverb, "You can't know how a man feels until you have walked a mile in his moccasins."

Chapter Five

Hard Core Unemployed

If the charge is made that George Butler is not the typical blue collar worker, it would be silly to attempt to defend him on that score, because nobody wants to be considered "typical", a part of a monolith, with no distinguishing marks or unique qualities. But it must be said that Butler's experience at Republic Steel, with a few minor changes, a few omissions, a few additions, could have been and still could be the experience of a goodly number of blue collar workers in any number of workplaces. Speaking simply and baldly, and without quoting doctrine or repeating slogans, one could say that while blue collar workers as a whole, typically, have a tough time making it, George Butler is a witness that if you come from the Black ghetto and are lucky, or unlucky, enough to be classified as "hard core unemployed", you will have it tougher than other blue collar workers.

George Butler was walking east on sixty-third street, a main artery of Chicago's Black ghetto. The elevated CTA tracks cast fluttering patchworks of sunlight, resembling prison bars, along the concrete sidewalks, and the street was strangely abandoned for a mid-afternoon. Usually, it teemed with shoppers, peddlers, dealers, joyseekers, escapees from crowded tenements. But today, *August 28, 1963,* a halt was called, all the stops were pulled, a period of rest, a moment of meditation. In every pool hall, tavern, lunch room, chicken shack, juke joint, gas station, bowling alley, people had gathered in groups around the television tubes, nodding silently to Dr. Martin Luther King's kindling sermon, *I Have a Dream,* as it was being delivered in contrapuntal tones from the foot of the Abraham Lincoln monument in Washington, D.C.

George Butler, a young man not yet sixteen, his face the color and grain of finely fashioned leather, dressed self-consciously in a white tee shirt and dark jeans, and wearing a red beret at just the right angle on his slender head, stopped and joined one of the groups at a cleaning shop near Stony Island Avenue, to watch and to listen and in some way, to share in the dream of Martin Luther King.

The "conscience of America," it was agreed, had gathered in the nation's Capitol, 250,000 strong, clergy, teachers, students, librarians, social workers, President Kennedy's own staff, artists, writers, Snicks, socialists, communists, do-gooders, and a few, damn few, blue collar workers, despite the later claims of international union officials.

It isn't a simple matter for a blue collar worker to take off and join a demonstration, unless his union promotes it, authorizes it, and finances it. An absence from work for reasons not approved by the company or union could get a worker into plenty of trouble.

(Except for a token delegation from the United Auto Workers Union—whose president, Walter Reuther, in his established position as a liberal friend of the Black people, pleaded with the leaders of the civil rights movement to cancel the march to avoid embarrassing the Kennedy administration—and for a few "left" union groups and dissident caucuses within the labor movement, union members and leaders were conspicuous by their absence from the march to Washington on August 28, 1963. They felt uncomfortable with the

"outsiders", the theoreticians, the militant slogans, the irrepressible rank and file character of the civil rights movement.

(Word filtered down from David J. MacDonald, then president of the Steelworkers Union, never as adept as Walter
Reuther in assessing political moods, that the March for Jobs
and Freedom was not his cup of tea, and Joseph Germano, his
union director in Chicago, spelled it out "loud and clear" that
the march to Washington was "not Labor's way. Our union
leaders have powerful friends and lobbyists in Washington,
and union members have no need to come to the Capitol.")

Butler saw it and heard it in the little shop on Stony Island.
"I have a dream . . . I have a dream . . . I have a dream that
one day this nation will rise up and live out the true meaning
of its creed . . . so let freedom ring . . . let freedom ring!"

The prophet of the civil rights movement, fitly a figure of
immortality, laid bare the pain and oppression of life for
Blacks in America, and the crowds in Washington wept openly and roared furiously from the depths of their centuries of
cruelty. Not since Eugene V. Debs and Franklin D. Roosevelt
did a troubled people hang on so tightly to the words of an
American orator.

George Butler grinned from ear to ear, and he whispered, to
nobody in particular, "Amen!" or it could have been "right
on!"

And then he felt, but paid no attention to a sweaty hand
gripping his bare arm, tighter and tighter. He didn't turn. He
kept his eyes on the television, not to miss a single word, waiting for the hand to be gone. He felt himself being pulled and
encircled, and a handcuff was snapped tight on his wrist.
Within minutes he was riding in a squad car with a Chicago
policeman on each side of him, headed for the Prairie Avenue
police station.

This wasn't his first ride in a police car. A ride to the police
station is a common experience for a young man on sixty-third
street, and Butler's prime reaction was one of irritation that
he was missing Dr. King's sermon.

(It has been reported that fifty per cent of all Black youth born in Philadelphia are arrested at least once before they reach the age of nineteen. The percentage on Chicago has never been reported, but it is highly unlikely that the "city of the broad shoulders" is behind the "city of brotherly love," at least in this respect.)

The red beret Butler was wearing pegged him a member of a southside street gang that had no clout at the Prairie Avenue police station. The beret, in itself, was grounds for being shoved in a police car, frisked, pummeled, questioned, and otherwise banished from the protection of the Constitution of the United States.

At the police station it was evident that Martin Luther King's sermon had very little impact. The radio was tuned to more pressing matters—police calls about shootings, beatings, accidents, heart attacks, fires, burglaries, but nothing about dreams.

Butler protested that he had done nothing, and there was no reason for his being picked up by the police, but nobody listened to him. It was all subdued, routine, and business-like. Not unfriendly, but distant, without the drama or bustle of police shows seen on television. A spectator could hardly make out what was happening. A short, red-faced man with crooked teeth and a smelly cigar stuck his head in Butler's face and said, "Yah, that's the one. That's the nigger that held the gun."

Nobody found a gun. Nobody found any loot, There were no witnesses or fingerprints to tie him to a crime. There had been a robbery on sixty-third street by what was described as two black youths in ski masks, and Butler was the first unattached black youth the police saw.

Butler had nobody to speak for him, nobody to swear he was innocent, nobody to establish a defense. He knew he was entitled to a phone call, but he had no one to call. He lived with his mother, but she was away.

Abandoning all hope, Butler did what he later recognized

as a foolish move. He tried to run from the police station, shouting his innocence. He jumped over rows of chairs, past a handful of policemen, and dove for the door. But a burly policeman wrestled him to the floor. He was locked up over night and held for Boys Court.

Now he faced the charge, in addition to that of armed robbery, of "resisting arrest" and "assault" against a police officer.

Justice was never so swift. In Chicago judges have been known for over-zealousness, and the Illinois Courts Commission recently "reprimanded" Judge Robert Sulski for sentencing a black defendant before the witnesses had an opportunity to testify—in the tradition of the old western movie—hang 'em first, and then the trial.

The "public defender" assigned to Butler fit the classic description of a "walking violation of the Sixth Amendment right to counsel." The armed robbery charge was dropped, but the "assault on a police officer" stuck. The judge did his meanest shit, and sent Butler up for one year at St. Charles. Three hundred and sixty five days was a lot of time for being caught listening to Dr. King's dream.

The venerable Black poet, Langston Hughes, asks:

What happens to a dream deferred?
Does it dry up
Like a raisin in the sun?
Or fester like a sore–
And then run?

George Butler came from the streets, where dreams have a terribly short span, and nobody bothers to check what happens to them. Getting through the day on an even keel, not the secret of a dream, is the matter to be mastered. Becoming an inmate of St. Charles was scarcely a turn in his life, so many of his friends had landed at the same reformatory. He had lived with this haunting future for half his young life, like young people in other communities might try to escape a dismal summer vacation with stuffy parents. It seemed there was no escape.

Though it is commonly believed that St. Charles and other such correctional institutions are nasty training schools for crime, they are actually, according to more sophisticated inmates, highly overrated. There are ghetto streets in Chicago and other urban centers that rate a good deal higher, with better instruction, more opportunity for on-the-job training, and a more certain future. These correctional institutions are filled with *losers.* Anyone contemplating a successful career in crime could do far better staying out of them and dig into the careers of the street-wise directors of Gulf Oil, Lockheed Aircraft, Tenneco, General Electric, I.T. & T., to name only a few of many scores who were caught "with a smoking gun" and never spent a day in a corrective institution.

George Butler did easy time and stayed real loose. If it could be said of anyone that "he beat the system," it can be said of Butler. He obeyed all the rules of St. Charles reformatory, shrugged off the hustlers, the punks and the pushers, dodged the psychiatric social worker who tried to poke his nose into his life, shared the warmth and fantasies of his snug community, and held on tightly to all his physical, mental and emotional belongings.

He came out of St. Charles the day he reached sixteen, a little taller, a bit sturdier, favoring his right shoulder which he had broken in an accident and didn't seem to heal properly, but with no other distinguishing marks that a term in prison or even a "boys school" such as St. Charles commonly suggests. It seems that these institutions exact their major toll from individuals whose careers have become interrupted or seriously damaged, or who will return to a community that will reject them, or whose own image of themselves has been diminished. But a childhood in the ghetto, nourished in overwhelming terror, often makes survivors tougher and braver and wiser.

Butler returned to do what he had been doing before he was arrested. Not much of anything, except to attend school off and on. Turned sixteen, he was finished with school. The rule in Chicago that school is compulsory until eighteen, like so many other rules and laws, was overlooked in the Black ghetto. He was too old for school and too young for work. He lived with his mother on welfare, watched over by his parole officer and social worker, and when he became eighteen, and old enough to work he discovered, first hand, that if the right to a job at eighteen was indeed a law, it was another one of those that weren't enforced in the ghetto.

(In the book, *Eleanor: the Years Alone,* the author, Joseph Lash, tells of Mrs. Roosevelt's frustration, as a United Nations delegate in 1947, that her own government refused to support a UN resolution guaranteeing full employment as a human right. The more sophisticated United States delegates patiently explained to Mrs. Roosevelt how a free society could become embroiled in a mess of troubles if the people considered employment a right. Twitted by the Soviet delegate for her opposition to the resolution, she replied, chastely, "The society in which everyone works is not necessarily a free society and may indeed be a slave society." The U.S. delegates made a big fuss over the word *guarantee,* and finally supported the resolution after it was changed to read *promote* full employment. It was the best the leaders of the free world could offer.)

Four White House administrations later, in 1962, a federal program to promote (not guarantee) employment in high unemployment areas was established under the *Manpower Development and Training Act,* which George Butler, with the help of his parole officer, social worker and precinct captain became a beneficiary of.

It was a program designed to train *hard core unemployed* for jobs that selected industries, in a spirit of social service, agreed to offer them. *Hard core unemployed* were men and women who would ordinarily be passed up if they applied for a job, even if there was an opening. They were people who had disqualifying marks all over their persons—X-rated—no work record, no references, no credit, bad neighborhood, bad coloring, police record, and dozens of other markings that employment supervisors are trained to sniff out.

Under the federal law, eligibility requirements for the *hard core* program were: "poor persons who do not have suitable employment and who are either (1) school drop-outs, (2) under 22 years of age, (3) over 45 years of age, (4) handicapped, or (5) subject to special obstacles to employment." Number 5 (5) was, of course, circumspect terminology for Black ghetto, though it could also mean Chicano.

George Butler was eminently qualified under (1), (2), and (5) for the government-industry hard core program. He signed all the papers for the government, was interviewed by the industry representative, and was well along the road to become a trainee for a job at the Republic Steel plant in South Chicago.

When one thinks of trainees for industry, there comes to mind the jobs requiring special knowledge and skills—electricians, machinists, pipe fitters, welders. But, the hard core program of training, which was to be three months of school, followed by nine months on-the-job training, emphatically excluded education for skilled jobs. It was designed that, after the schooling, the trainee would enter the bottom job, the lowest paid job, generally that of laborer in the plant, which would in no way compete with the jobs of the normal, non-X rated, deserving employees hired in accordance with accepted personnel practices.

Educational corporations with extravagant claims to expertise, emerged in every industrial center to cadge contracts with industries for the training of their hard core workers. An Indianapolis corporation, the *Board for Fundamental Education*, with a forceful endorsement from the National Association of Manufacturers, satisfied the international union and the steel corporations that it possessed pedagogical secrets unknown to adult education faculties licensed by state and county boards of education, and secured the contract to train the hard core unemployed for the steel industry.

Observing the training classes at Republic Steel, one promptly perceived that the instructors and staff were as vulgar and dishonest a group as ever claimed professional status. But, it must be considered, the entire project was based on the hokum that ghetto youth were unemployed because of their own deficiencies, their inability to fit into the workplace. A twelve week course of training was supposed to wipe out these deficiencies, and ready them for the workplace.

In 1968, the year George Butler was admitted to the program, the U.S. Labor Department gave Republic Steel $658,000 to train 112 hard core workers for their plant in South Chicago. That amounts to $5,875 for each worker. How such sums are spent in a twelve week course of study is one of the questions never publicly answered. The Board for Fundamental Education didn't get all of it. The hard core trainee didn't get a red penny of it—their weekly compensation was paid from other taxpayer funds. There was manifestly an enormous profit in the business of training hard core unemployed for industry.

If this were its only fault, it might be passed over. But the facts show that the entire hard core program, a sacred cow of the Great Society, never questioned or evalutated, was a cruel hoax and a betrayal of the ghetto youth.

George Butler was in a class where the instructors were teaching "remedial reading", though Butler read newspapers and magazines on a regular basis. It's true some couldn't read as well as Butler, but all the trainees were put in the same class regardless of reading levels. Everybody knows Blacks can't read! How can they understand written directives, make out the safety signs, understand instructions in the mill, if they can't read? That's what made them *hard core*. Right? Right!

After four weeks in the classroom, Butler, and some others,

too, were told they were ready to go into the mill and work on the job, and be paid the regular rate for their jobs exactly like any other worker in the mill. Butler was assigned to the 34 inch mill as a laborer. He figured he was ahead, being graduated early, and while he knew his government had paid for twelve weeks, that was none of his concern, and besides, he considered the time spent in the classroom a waste and a nuisance. He was more than ready for a full-time regular job. His muscles were happy and relaxed, and alive with a craving for arduous physical activity. He ached to lose himself in the comaraderie of the workplace. He ached for the even pattern of purposeful sleeping, rising, dressing, working, eating, loving.

He blended easily with the other workers in the 34 inch mill. There were no marks or signs on him declaring he was a hard core worker, rated "X". His status was to be kept secret and confidential, known only to supervision. He performed the full scope of the work of the laborer's job, after just a few minutes of instruction. He dressed the same, punched the clock like the others, was subject to all the rules, was controlled by all the practices and disciplines on absenteeism, work scheduling, safety equipment, horseplay, response to signals.

There was one ugly deformity, deeply rooted, and not immediately visible to the untrained eye, but it turned out to be vital. It was the cause of his downfall, and spread like a plague to attack every hard core worker wherever he or she happened to be. As is so often the case in social and organic life, the laying bare of a seemingly innocent blemish leads to a deep well-spring of insidious malignancy. Butler's experience is such a case.

Each hard core employee, when hired under the MDTA program, was (and is) required to sign what amounts to a "yellow dog contract", an all-but-forgotten term out of the bitter worker-employer conflicts of the nineteenth and early twentieth centuries. In the early days of labor organization in the United States, workers were coerced by employers into signing individual agreements pledging to abstain from union membership or support of union organization—viewed in labor relations as an agreement to become a *scab* during a strike, or, in any event, to reduce the worker to a more manageable state. Workers who signed such agreements were labeled by unionists of the time as "low down as a yellow dog," and the yellow dog contract survived as part of the rich lexicon of Labor terminology. The Norris-LaGuardia Act, passed by Congress in 1932, made such agreements illegal. But, like other laws that weren't enforced in the Black ghetto, the Norris-LaGuardia Act didn't protect George Butler.

The hard core worker, upon being accepted, was required to sign a statement reading, "I understand that I am being hired conditionally under the Special Employment Program as established by the Chicago District and Local 1033, United Steelworkers of America (or the industrial District or Local Union which was applicable) by their Memorandum of Agreement. . . . I therefore agree that I will actively pursue the course of study prescribed for me by the Company and understand that I will be a probationary employee for a minimum of six (6) months from the day I am hired and *there is a possible maximum probationary period of twelve (12) months from the date I am hired. I understand that I may be discharged from the Company during the probationary period, as solely determined by the Company, and that neither the Company nor the Union may be held responsible for such discharge."* (Emphasis added.)

By signing this statement the hard core worker surrendered to one hundred years of defeated labor, and the companies regained a victory they had lost by the Norris-LaGuardia Act.

Eventually word spread that these hard core workers were dangerous cats from the ghetto, who carried guns and knives, were on drugs, were radical Black power advocates, that they were paid more than the regular workers, that they didn't pay union dues, that they could never be fired, that a jail record was a prerequisite for getting into the program—the whole warped butt of privelege-endangered newcomers.

The Company made a half-hearted effort to win approval for its hard core employees. It invited the union officers and a number of selected supervisors to attend orientation conferences, where MDTA literature was distributed, a representative of the U.S. Labor Department spoke, the Industrial Relations counsellor was serving coffee, and never in the memories of the assembled unionists had the rhetoric of racial reconciliation flowed so thick. It all seemed so stiff and apologetic. The program was explained as a social welfare program for the Black ghetto. "If we don't give 'them' jobs, we have to support 'them' anyhow."

Butler stayed real loose at Republic Steel—an art he learned at St. Charles Reformatory. He had the advantage of an open youthful face, unbounded energy, not being tied to family or social obligations, and, this was most important, he was always willing to "stay over" another eight hours in the event a worker from the following turn reported off. Such dependability was highly valued by the company. Butler never said "no" to an offer to stay over "another eight." Well, hardly ever. There was one job he shrank from, and it was no secret. If staying over meant filling the job of *stamper*, Butler would, regretfully, turn it down. Ever since his accident at St. Charles his right shoulder gave him trouble, and swinging a sledgehammer, which the stamper's job required, gave him pain. Obligingly, Butler wasn't asked, except in a dire emergency, when it was impossible to get anyone to fill the job. All steel in the 34 inch mill had to be stamped with the heat number on each bar. Sometimes Butler would give in, but usually he begged off. No sweat. Butler was a good company man.

At one point in his remarkable mill career, he became something of a celebrity. The word was that his brother was a successful blues singer in concert at the Auditorium—a measure of status even among those who didn't dig the blues—and

George Butler never went out of his way to comment on the relationship. Being the brother of someone with a big name seemed to have advantages over being a hard core worker in one's own right. White workers in the department who never as much as said "Hy 'ya!" now would ask him to join them for coffee. Some even made bad jokes about the merits of kielbasse over soul food. They exchanged tall stories about their inter-racial affairs with women, how much they paid for their cars, how much they won at the track, their iron-handed control of their wives, and all those matters that emphasized their mutuality of interests rather than their exclusiveness. The foremen also treated him with extraordinary respect.

He was happy as long as nobody gave him a hard time about doing the stamper's job. It's always risky to say "no" to a supervisor in a plant. Somehow it's never completely forgotten. It is commonly suspected that all such refusals are written down and entered into the workers *personal file*. In most modern institutions today, in the family, the school, the government, the church, the courts, there has developed a tolerance for dissent, but least so in the workplace. Neither Dr. Spock or the ACLU has any standing in a steel mill. "Insubordination" is a term heard more frequently at Republic Steel than at the Fifth Army headquarters. The union advises its members to obey all orders given by their superiors, even if they violate the union contract—and a grievance may be filed later. "A steel mill is not a debating society," an arbitrator ruled in a landmark decision upholding the company.

As everyone knows, sooner or later a false reputation is found out. Butler suspected he saw signs that the rumor about his brother as a bigtime blues singer was wearing thin. If somebody had a rich brother would he be living in the ghetto? Would he be riding the busses to work? Would he be so hungry for overtime? Butler is a common name—hundreds are in the phone directory and some don't have phones. Butler had never said straight out that it was his brother, he merely smiled when it was mentioned. It was like a kid who boasted in the winter time what a great swimmer he was, and in the summer about his smart skating, but no one had ever seen him in the lake, or on the rink, and when the other kids finally tricked him out to the Lake Michigan forty-seventh street beach, he sank to the bottom like a lead bob. That's the way it was with George Bulter, though he had only half-contrived it, the brother who was supposed to be a famous blues singer, was, for all practical purposes, dead and buried. But for reasons that went far deeper, George Butler, not only George Butler, but all his hard core cohorts too, were lined up for a similar fall, out the gate, back to the welfare rolls.

It was all so neat, like a kiss-off in a godfather movie.

The regularly assigned stamper was on vacation, and the foreman asked Butler every day to fill the stamper's job, and every day he turned it down. At the end of the week the foreman told him, "I have to give you a day off, for refusing to work as directed." He was glad to get the day off, as he had been putting in a lot of overtime and his shoulder was hurting.

When he returned to work the foreman told him "the boss wants you to stamp today." Butler shook his head and pointed to his shoulder, and the foreman pulled a suspension notice from his pocket. It was already filled out—three days suspension—signed by the superintendent. Butler laughed, "You knew I wasn't going to do it, didn't you."

Instead of going directly home, Butler stopped at the union office. Hard core workers were members of the union, contrary to rumors. There he was told the union couldn't do anything for him, since there was a written agreement that the company can fire hard core workers any time until they have put in a year of service. "If you can hang on for another couple of weeks (it was five days to be exact) you'll have a year in, and then the union can protect you. But not before. So just watch your step for the next couple of weeks."

Butler wasn't aware, since he had no way of knowing what

went on in other parts of the sprawling plant, that he was one of the last few of the one hundred and twelve hard core workers who started off with him as a trainee, who was still working in the plant. They had all been fired, under the provisions of their yellow dog agreement.

When he returned from his three day discipline, and before he had a chance to change his clothes, he was told by his foreman that the superintendent wanted him in his office. There, without raising his head, the superintendent read off a list of "personal reports"—*failure to work as directed* (with the dates of violation), *insubordination* (with dates), *excessive absenteeism* (undocumented), *poor workmanship* (citing normal stamper's errors), *failure to satisfactorily complete the twelve weeks of schooling for trainees* (!)—it was all there in black on white (or would it be a bad joke to say *white on black*?). The superintendent handed him his discharge notice, to take effect immediately, five days before he would be released from his yellow dog contract, and told him he wasn't "suitable" for work in a steel mill.

One can't help theorize that Richard Wright's *Bigger Thomas* hadn't come very far in forty years. In so many ways he was still dispossessed and disinherited, still excluded and subject to special rules, X-rated and off limits in so many jobs, and, if working, it was so often under a yellow dog contract without union protection.

"I made a discovery," said Richard Wright, lecturing in 1940 at a Harlem public library, "that Bigger Thomas was not black all the time; he was white too, and there was literally millions of him everywhere."

George Butler put it differently to his superintendent when he took the discharge notice from him. "You were after my black ass from the minute I came here."

Chapter Six

Rank and File

The road from Osceola, Arkansas, north to the sprawling steelmaking plants on Chicago's far south side, is not a direct or well-travelled drive, though it wasn't by chance or loss of direction that the Lyons family, in 1958, with all their belongings loaded on their patched-up, overhauled Dodge truck, headed for that fabled city. They had heard from most reliable sources, including kinfolks who had made it, that "if you can't make it in Chicago, you can't make it anywhere." It was a church-going city of opportunity, jobs, good living, new songs and high wages. A common laborer in the Chicago mills was then known to earn a hundred dollars a week, while in Osceola, if there was a job to be had, it wouldn't pay half that.

For the Lyons family, who owned no home and no land, but lived as tenant farmers, under arrangements that provided only the essentials for the body and soul, the good life, the life they were seeking in Chicago, was, above everything else, an opportunity for the youngest son, James, ready for high school, to go on and become a man of the law, even a judge. This is what they cared about most. It was a resolution that was weighed and measured and discussed within the family over and over, and James' teachers in school, the deacons of the church, and even the landowner James helped with the crops, concurred that James was going to be somebody some day. At another time, when Malcolm X, according to his *Autobiography*, told his teacher, Mr. Ostrowski, he wanted to become a lawyer, he was advised, "A lawyer—that's no realistic goal for a Nigger."

With the good wages that could be earned in Chicago by the father and the two elder sons, James would go through high school and college to become a lawyer. Chicago wasn't New York. James wasn't Malcolm. Nineteen-sixty wasn't nineteen-forty.

They settled in their cramped Chicago home, an aged frame house, far away from the ghetto, far from the gangs and the crime, far from the broken families on ADC, in the mill community known as South Chicago, adjacent to the "Big Mill" of the United States Steel Corporation. It was one of a small cluster of company-type homes occupied chiefly by Black blue collar workers, walled in by the larger white ethnic community. The homes were all equally and evenly layered with the dark steel dust expelled from the mill stacks, and they were surrounded by rail tracks with perpetual lines of freight trains clamoring to be loaded and moved. There was a pervasive blight in the area, due to the recurrent rumors that it was to be razed to make way for the expansion of the "Big Mill."

The residents were remarkably integrated, racially, in contrast with other areas of Chicago which had developed a ghastly pattern of vigilante violence towards Blacks as neighbors. (The fire-bombings in the *Trumbull Park* federal housing project, next door to the Wisconsin Steel Company, was the most publicized example in that period. Not publicized, however, was that the bombs were crudely manufactured by employees in the steel plants, without interference from plant supervision, or that the weekly news bulletin published by the mob—the *South Deering News*—was brought into the plants by the plant guards and supervisory employees).

Integrated housing was established in this U. S. Steel community during the 1919 steel strike when the company, to break the strike, imported Blacks from the South. Here, James enrolled at Bowen High School, drastically changed, after the war. A middle class community had sprung up during the war within the Bowen school district, and the school responded appropriately with an enriched curriculum, and what amounted to a benign neglect of the sons and daughters of the blue collar workers. James, in his single-minded pursuit of learning, competed capably. He was on the school debating team and the dramatic club. He played Othello in a community performance at the school auditorium, and a handfull of troublemakers booed and hooted, but there was a loud self-conscious applause from many in the audience who felt betrayed by this uncouth display of racism. It was a thrilling night for the devoted Lyons family, even if it hadn't been a dramatic hit. James' speaking voice, a rich baritone, they observed, was ideally suited for his chosen profession of Law.

As happens to so many teens from blue collar families, commonly perceived in social researchers' notebooks, as symptomatic of "low-esteem" or "feelings of personal inadequacy," James became impatient with school by the time of his senior year, impatient with the long span of childhood that the school affected, wanting to go beyond childhood and be the man he was sure he was ready to be. He had lost his boyhood before he left Osceola. He had worked like a man on the rented land, chopping cotton and hoeing potatoes, and it was too late now to live the role of a juvenile, detached from the world, dependent on parents and older brothers for fulfillment of his needs. Had it not been for the desperate pleas of his family, and what he considered his own solemn vows, he would have ended his school career at that point. But he coasted along, and graduated with his class in 1962 at the age of nineteen, and was accepted for the freshman class by the University of Illinois.

As the summer days passed, the state university receded further and further from his sights. His older brothers had married and were raising their own families. Two new brothers had been borne to the Lyons family. The only income was his father's paycheck from United States Steel, a fair wage when he could work overtime, but lately reduced by cutbacks in the plant, short work-weeks, and sickness. It took careful managing to stretch it through the week. (If it is true that the poor can get through the university if they really want it, that there are scholarships, loans, part-time work opportunities and other forms of patronage available to seriously motivated poor, James wasn't let in on the secret).

Instead of the state university downstate, James enrolled at Crane—a community junior college in the city—where tuition was nominal, and his only expenses would be books, clothes, transportation, and the like, which he could take care of with a part-time job.

In his first semester at Crane, James studied accounting, public speaking, Spanish and English, courses he was advised would prepare him for law school. He was itching to begin the study of law, but, of course, he couldn't change the rules that required four years in a liberal arts college and then three years of law. Was this rule, again, something like his high school experiences, to prolong childhood, to keep him removed from society? Not only Blacks in their prime of life were diminished to "boy!" but whites too were being held back from normal manhood. If all went well, James would be twenty-six before he was finished with law school—pretty old to be living in the crowded tenement with his parents and brothers, living off the labor of his father. (His father often said, "When you're Black, age doesn't make much difference. Opportunity doesn't come in a flash for our people.")

It's curious, that when the subtle complexities of life cannot be deciphered and resist all logical solutions, an event happens in one uncommited instant that delivers the master key. James got married, and a child was on the way.

There had to be a new way of life. On his own. A full-time job, a place for them to live. No more dependence on his father, God love him, and no more postponing of manhood. Attending school at night, they calculated, would take about eight years to graduate, and law school at night would be another seven or eight years. Is thirty-seven the right age to start a career in law? It's been done.

James applied at Republic Steel for a job in the accounting department—something that wouldn't be so tiring and would make it easier for him to study. He mentioned his accounting courses at Crane Junior College, but it didn't make any impression. He was offered a job as a *straddle-truck operator* at $2.69 an hour, and he said he would take it. (Had he then been hired as a clerk in the accounting department it would have been a break-through for Blacks).

Operating a straddle-truck had its advantages. It was a lot better than a laborer's or janitor's job—the job that newly hired employees in the mills were supposed to start at. It was a Class 10 job, in a scale from 1 to 32. At the time, James wasn't aware that this too was a break-through. He was the first Black to be a straddle truck operator at this plant. It had been an all-white department, and James came to the employment office on the very day management decided to "integrate" the straddle truck operators. James saw other good sides to the job. Nobody would be breathing down his back. The straddle truck operator is caged in a cab high off the ground, similar to a crane or shovel operator, and receives his instructions from a dispatcher by radio. He travels from department to department, from shipping dock to shipping dock, to gather up and transport steel billets, bars and ingots to various stations within the plant for either shipment or further processing. A fleet of straddle-trucks are in continuous motion, carrying their loads without let-up.

James had planned to tell the employment office that he was going to night school and would like a day shift job. But the atmosphere when he hired in didn't seem right for setting down conditions. It seemed to him they weren't too happy about hiring him at all, and it's easy to queer an opportunity by having a special problem. Though it was a year of economic prosperity, and Lyndon Johnson, in his presidential inaugural address said, "the liberation of man (is) our goal today," jobs were still hard to find.

On shift work, he unavoidably missed about half his classes at Crane. Rotating work schedules make a hunter's stew out of any life pattern in relation to school, church, clubs, family or union. Under the most favorable circumstances he would be compelled to be absent from all his classes one third of the time (when he worked the three to eleven, afternoon, shift) and frequently he had to choose between work and school when overtime opportunities arose on his job. Unless the company put him on a steady day shift he would miss too much school to make it worthwhile. The company told him it wouldn't be fair to the other operators, and that settled it for James. He decided to postpone school for a while, and pick it up again at a more favorable time.

He enjoyed living a more normal life as a worker, he welcomed the fellowship of the men in the plant, liked the way they talked and lived, and he gradually developed close friends among the young Black workers who were coming into the plant in increasing numbers. He was uncomfortable in his position as a "token Black" on a white man's job. He suspected he fitted into some unwritten integration agreement which he had no part in making. However, in a short period of a year the straddle-truck operator job ceased being a "white job." It became a "Black job." This was the way industry's equal employment program, under the Civil Rights Act of 1964, would often progress.

The rules of racial discrimination in industry yielded slowly and grudgingly under the pressure of the civil rights movement. All about him, James observed attitudes and incidents that troubled him. A recently-hired Black straddle-truck operator, James' good friend, Ben Chaney, was fired because his truck broke down in the middle of the turn, and instead of notifying the dispatcher, as was standard procedure, Ben notified the garage. It was a mistake he freely acknowledged. It was his first experience with a breakdown, and he goofed. But he didn't believe he should have been fired for it. Neither did James.

James wasn't experienced on matters of company discipline. He, himself, had never been disciplined at work, and he had only an instinctive reaction to the company's approach as it effected Blacks. It's an intricate system in American industry, affecting blue collar workers of all races, though enforced unevenly, having its roots in the codes governing the indentured servants of colonial days in America. Collective bargaining has accomplished very little in altering the fundamental assumptions, attitudes and attachments of corporate employers concerning discipline in the workplace. The right to discipline its employees has been broadly conceded as an inalienable right of management, implicit in ownership of capital, a basic property of the productive process, a timeless relationship between worker and boss, and is solidly validated in most union contracts, in classical language stating that "the Company retains the exclusive rights to manage the business and the plants and to direct the working forces . . . including the right to hire, suspend or discharge for proper cause. . .". The quotes are from the Steelworkers Union contract, but it is substantially the same in most union contracts, and though it sounds innocent enough, it is under this contractual right that employees are given time off, sometimes up to a year, or are discharged from employment, without benefit of the rights citizens enjoy under the due process of our legal system.

Grievances protesting disciplines may be filed, and they constitute the overwhelming majority of complaints of blue collar workers. Such grievances are most usually settled in favor of the company before they are processed. The sheer numbers of disciplines makes them impractical to oppose within the machinery of the union grievance procedure. A grievanceman in one single division of the Republic plant, covering six hundred employees, handled one hundred and sixty-five suspensions over a six month period. Allowing for repeaters, one of every four employees in the division was punished with "time off" for alleged infraction of rules. Edward Sadlowski, when he was president of the local union at the big mill of U. S. Steel in South Chicago, reported 3400 disciplines in a single year at that plant of 10,000 reported 3400 disciplines in a single year at that plant of 10,000 employees—one third of the work force punished for breaking the rules. If the adult population of the nation were subject to a comparable system of disciplines, it would translate, roughly, into 45 million citations per year!

It agitated James that Ben Chaney was fired for such a flimsy cause, not only because Ben was his friend, but his intrinsic nature was to become drawn into social controversy and to dig for the hidden truth. Talk flowed freely among the Black straddle-truck operators that Ben had been "sold down the river" by the union, that the company had it in for him because he had previously filed a grievance alleging racial discrimination, and there was no denying that the union wasn't over-zealous in taking on the company on discrimination grievances.

James went to the union office—his first direct contact with the union—to inquire about Ben Chaney, and though he was treated friendly enough, he wasn't satisfied the union officers understood the seriousness of the discharge. He wasn't satisfied the union was aware of the discrimination and the humiliation the Black workers faced, or was it that they had overlooked these conditions for so long that they considered them normal.

Unattended wounds begin to fester, and it reached the point where a group of straddle truck operators walked, or, as the company told it, "stormed" into the superintendent's office and demanded a meeting to discuss *overtime distribution*. Notorious throughout the plant for his reputation as a rough, no-nonsense steelmaster who ran his department like a ship's captain, the superintendent became visibly ruffled by this unheard-of confrontation with his operators. He sternly announced he was leaving for a meeting with his department foremen. The operators raised their voices and shouted for him to stay until he heard them out, and several blocked the doorway. James faced him directly, and held up his hand. "Just one minute is all we want." The others immediately became silent, a sort of plebiscite electing James as their spokesman. The superintendent sat on the edge of his steel desk and listened impatiently while James told him the Black straddle truck operators were being discriminated against, and they wanted "equal distribution of overtime." The superintendent was apparently relieved that it was nothing more serious, and he readily agreed to sign an agreement giving every employee in the unit an equal share of the overtime work. In a department that was intending to go from all-white to all-Black, such an agreement was not momentous. But the manner of negotiating it was most unusual and it was a breach of the union contract. The union's grievance committeeman wasn't in on it. It was an activity of a *rank and file* breed—a term borrowed from the military, referring to the body of an organization, apart from its officers.

In the trade union, a *rank and file* worker is any member, other than an officer or functionary. And since there are relatively very few officers and functionaries in a union, the term *rank and file* would seem, on first impression, to have about as much meaning as the term citizen, Brother, Occupant, taxpayer. Aren't we all?

Not quite. Under the special circumstances of trade union development in the United States, different from the military, civic, academic, commercial, and, to some extent, religious organizations, opposition to the union leadership sprouted and grew from its earliest beginnings, taking the form of theoretical polemics, establishment of rival unions, expulsion of dissidents, hotly contested elections, the knocking together of heads, and assassinations. The opposition was generally led by union members who claimed they represented the *rank and file,* and were engaged in a moral crusade to dislodge the misleaders and to halt their sinful activities. Though all such movements weren't pure in heart, they were mainly responsible for curbing dishonesty internally, defending the economic interests of the membership, and organizing the unorganized workers. *Rank and fileism,* during the heydey of the IWW, became synonomous with militancy, democratic unionism, political awareness, class consciousness.

Since the 1930s and the organization of the basic industries by the CIO, which employed great numbers of volunteers, non-paid activists, and plant workers on the job, the *rank and filer* has been given a recognized status in many unions. So much so, that shrewd aspirants for union office will seek to run on a rank and file slate whether or not they have established any kind of reputation as a rank and filer, somewhat as modern self-proclaimed "populists" seeking political office.

The late Walter Reuther was a rank and filer when he went into an automobile plant and helped organize the UAW, but after he became president of the union, and was in a battle with George Meany for the leadership of the AFL-CIO, his claims as a rank and filer didn't carry much weight. "The young radicals of yesterday are the middle aged pork-choppers of today" has enough truth in it to convince the skeptics of the labor movement, but nobody would deny that there have been many notable exceptions.

The company reacted swiftly to this rank and file activity in the department.

"Are we going to have to put up wih a bunch of radicals storming the superintendents' offices with complaints? Is that the way the grievance procedure is going to work? Can't you control your own men?" were the rhetorical questions the company's industrial relations counsellor fired at the local union president, as if they had been scrupulously rehearsed, as indeed they were, being the identical questions fired on a quite similar occasion, when rank and file activity of the electrical line gang, protesting, this time, "excessive" and "compulsory" overtime (twelve hour shifts, without let-up, for weeks on end) was effectively rebuffed, in the manner of a prison riot, by suspending every member of the line gang from three to thirty days, according to the degree of participation.

The union president assured the company that James and his confederates acted without union authorization, and that everything would be done to preserve the integrity of the grievance procedure.

The company frequently calls upon the union to help discipline the employees, and modern unions have accepted this role. Some unions, notably the building trades, include supervisory employees, with power to hire or fire, as members of the same local union as those they boss on the job. Such practices have provoked some circles of liberalism and leftism to denounce unions as the chief obstacle to workers' liberation, and the railings and denunciations formerly reserved for bosses and capitalists have been turned loose on unions.

Inevitably, James was invited to come to the local union office for a meeting. They wanted to know what he was up to. They explained, respectfully enough, that he wasn't authorized to represent or advise the men in the plant, that grievancemen were elected and appointed to handle the members' problems, and that he was getting the union into trouble with the company. The company could fire him for what he had done at the superintendent's office. "However, if you want to be active in the union, we can appoint you to a committee. Would you like that?"

James answered that he was interested in helping his people, and there was a lot of racial discrimination in the plant. And, from what he had seen, he believed Ben Chaney was given a rotten deal.

"We did all we could for him . . . you don't know the facts . . . you're listening to latrine lawyers who want to tear down this union . . . Ben is an agitator . . . we warned him to straighten out," yelled the union spokesman.

He left the union meeting feeling empty and unfulfilled. He hadn't accomplished anything, and didn't know what his next step would be. He knew he wasn't ready to be appointed to some union committee, until he got to the bottom of what he considered "rotten conditions in the plant." He had heard some pretty harsh words condemning the local union and its officers by white as well as Black steelworkers, and there was a widespread suspicion that "the union was in the company's pocket." But, on the other hand, he had also seen the union speaking out, on several occasions, for the rights of the workers. It wasn't that simple. Anyhow, between his job, his new family, and the class he had registered for at Crane Junior college, there didn't seem to be much time for other activities. He felt he should be studying more, and taking a fuller schedule of classes.

But, in the world of the blue collar worker, as in everyone's, the best laid plans go astray and the neatest dreams are overwhelmed by uncontrollable events. In James' life, it was an act of Congress.

In 1964 President Lyndon Johnson signed the Civil Rights Act, which included the ambiguous *Title VII* establishing an Equal Employment Opportunities Commission (EEOC) charged with investigating and settling complaints of *"discrimination based on race, color, religion, sex or national origin in hiring, apprenticeship, compensation, and terms, conditions or privileges of employment . . .".*

And the following year, a contest, unusual for the trade union movement, to elect the international president of the United Steelworkers of America, produced the most profound stirrings among the Black steelworkers. This was the first serious union election to give them a chance to bargain their voting strength. The incumbent president, David J. MacDonald, a woefully pompous bureaucrat, with almost no links to, or understanding of, the Black steelworkers, boasted on a national television "talk show" that the Black steelworkers regarded him "as the great white father," and that he had done away with racial discrimination in the mills. I. W. Abel, the opposition candidate, campaigned skillfully to win support from the Black steelworkers, and to the extent that the replacement of MacDonald by Abel as president of the Union was more than a "palace revolution," the weightiest factor was the activities of the Black steelworkers.

The effect of these events was that for the first time in the history of James' union, a "Black Caucus" became legitimate. Previously, any grouping within the union (and this was true of most unions) was fiercely condemned as a form of "dual unionism" to be pitilessly crushed—usually under the guise of a "red threat to undermine the union." But after the thaw of the civil rights act and the upheaval of an election contest for international office, Black Caucuses in local unions all over the country were springing up like mushrooms.

James Lyons became secretary of the Black caucus in his local union. It wasn't an office one ran for, nor did the caucus have any official status, other than being tolerated. James attended its first meeting at a YMCA conference room, and someone asked him if he would take minutes. He agreed. Them someone stood up at the head table and said, "we need a chairman." It seemed, whoever he was, that he had been the chief convener of the meeting, and everyone insisted he *was* the chairman. The newly "elected" chairman immediately brought order and a sense of business to the meeting, and then asked for a vote on James Lyon for secretary. Everyone present knew about James, and he was unanimously elected.

In no formal sense could this procedure be described as democratic, but neither did anyone think someone was ramming something down their throat. Within the Black caucus, as with most union rank and file groupings in which reprisals are more likely than rewards, competition for leadership isn't strong. The one-man-one-vote principle isn't in full flower, and democratic procedure finds a level comparable to what might be expected among a group shipwrecked on an island.

(That such informality may, and often has, become a cover for the entrenchment of a burocracy or dictatorship, is a serious danger, and probably no group is more aware of this danger than the rank and file movements in the trade unions.)

The Black caucuses were loose associations that were evoked by the flagrant denial of equal rights to Blacks both inside the workplace and the union, but, in addition to this basic grievance, the caucuses brought together Blacks with varied motives and aims. They included some who aspired to regularly elected union office and wanted the support of the caucus. They also drew Blacks who viewed the union as hopelessly anti-Black and favored handling the problems of discrimination through other organizations such as PUSH, NAACP, or the United States Labor Department. There were some who had strong attachments to the labor movement and intended to improve its function by stamping out its racist practices. And still others who saw in the Black caucus a way "to get whitey."

In this broad scheme of purpose, James maintained a position that all and every means should be used to put the Black worker on an equal footing with the white. There wasn't a right way and wrong way, as far as he knew. Try different roads. See which takes you where you want to go. A sure way to lose your way is to get bogged down in family quarrels. You have to know who you are. If you're poor you're not a boss; if you're a sharecropper you're not a landlord; if you're a prisoner of war you're not a conquering officer; if you're a hospital patient you're not the mortician. You have to know who you are. If you're Black, you're not white, and if you don't believe it, listen to white man's talk in the mill when they think they're alone.

Whatever his point of view, James rapidly emerged as the spokesman for the Black caucus. He was the "hot line," the confessor, the advocate, the rank and file leader through whom Black steelworkers in the mill filtered their complaints and received counsel. Driving his straddletruck from department to department, he was easy to contact, and he learned how to keep his activities unnoticed by his supervision, and by the union, though he knew he was in danger.

(The International Union had a long history of opposition to any dissenting or rank and file movement within the organization. Such activities are approached as a serious disease, a cancer. In the 1940s, the steelworkers' first International president, Philip Murray, came down hard on those rank and file steelworkers who opposed the union's cold war accomodation, and he characterized his opposition as "a cancer to be excised." Murray's hand-picked successor, David J. MacDonald, in seeking to outlaw a candidate, Don Rarick, a mill hand who dared to run against him in 1958, implored the delegates assembled in convention to "rip this cancer out of your bowels." The next international president, I. W. Abel, at a 1974 conference of local union officials at the Shoreham Hotel in Washington, pleaded for support against the rank and file movement which opposed a no-strike agreement, and called it "a cancer in our midst that should be cleaned out." Any rank and file movement is diagnosed by the officialdom of unions as a radical disease, requiring radical surgery—to be "excised," "ripped out," "cleaned out.")

Shortly after I. W. Abel was elected international president of the Steelworkers Union, he made a highly publicized visit to the management of the Chicago works of Republic Steel— a public relations measure to counter the rumors that the new president was some kind of an insurgent planning to depart from the cozy pattern of "mutual trusteeship", established by his predecessors. The Black caucus decided it had a stake in the meeting, and two dozen Black steelworkers marched in picket line formation at the company office, requesting to be allowed to attend the meeting. Never in the memories of the company or union had anything like this happened. It was uncouth, disruptive, and probably violated the union constitution! "We want to tell you about discrimination in this plant," said James.

Abel was fresh from renowned service as a liberal advocate
on the National Commission on Civil Disorders, appointed by
President Johnson, and to be told about racial discrimination
by a rank and file worker appeared awkward, embarrassing,
difficult to handle. When presented with a list of "lily-white
departments" and jobs that were closed to Black workers, he
quoted from the most recent civil rights resolution passed at
the union's convention, that "our union has been devoted to
the priniciple of equality since it was founded . . .(and) the
USWA has diligently attempted to broaden job opportunities
years before the passage of federal civil rights legislation . . ."
The company officials quietly left the meeting while Abel was
conferring with his union brothers. It was not their way of
handling plant problems.

If the meeting accomplished nothing more, it firmly established James Lyons as a rank and file leader among his brothers and fellow workers, and pushed him along towards a new
assessment of his own goals.

Wasn't there anyone, he mused, who could shake up the
company, make it more human and decent, insist that it at
least live up to its end of the union contract? What's wrong
with union leaders? Could he, as a lawyer, some day, plead
Labor's cause in the courtroom, like Clarence Darrow or
Thurgood Marshall? Deep down, he began to have doubts
that his and his family's ambition for a law career was prac-
ticable. There were so many stubborn obstacles that had been
overlooked—shift work on the job, he wasn't getting any
younger, his wife was pregnant with a second child, and there
were all these problems and all these people in the mill that
were somehow depending on him. He had a prophetic hunch
that he really belonged in the mill, with his Brothers, in the
Black caucus, in the union. He had a talent and an understanding and a love for justice and equality, not inherited or
effortless as with some libertarians, not nicely honed and polished as with some professional do-gooders, but hammered
crudely into the framework of his life as a boy on the land in

Arkansas and, later, in the workplaces of South Chicago, where he saw injustice on a gigantic scale. He knew he would never desert his Brothers.

The local union elections were coming up, and a meeting of the Black caucus decided James should run for secretary, an office never held by a Black worker in the local union. The caucus believed that, with the support it could muster among the Black members of the union, coupled with additional numbers of white members who were dissatisfied with the entrenched leadership of the union and were attracted to James' style of militancy, a break-through was possible, and the Black workers in the plant would have an eloquent spokesman within the union. The local union leadership, with the view of strengthening its own chances for re-election, agreed to support James' candidacy in return for the support of the Black caucus. Politics is a well-studied art in the local unions, imitative of international union elections and of big city political machines.

There is nothing new to the observation that the nationally known leaders of the labor movement of our country, the AFL-CIO executive council, the heads of the international unions, the presidents of state and county labor federations, together with their salaried aids and staffs, are, in most respects, far removed from the blue collar workers who pay dues (checked off by the employer), march on picket lines, file grievances, face lay-off, and are subject to the discipline of the workplace. They have a different life-style, higher incomes, and have an easier, friendlier relationship with industry management and the political structure than what the blue collar worker has. The mass media, and, to an extraordinary degree, the schools of social science, in dealing with Labor, are not concerned with such differences. Labor is George Meany, or I. W. Abel, or Woodcock, or James Hoffa (even in death). The Union is in a many-storied building in

Washington, Detroit, Pittsburgh, or Chicago. Labor's activities are at Congressional hearings, political conventions, press conferences, and the highly-publicized collective bargaining table, negotiating a contract for the men and women in the workplace.

But the local union of workers inside the workplace, in terms of their working conditions and earnings, in terms of the worker given a three day suspension for violating a work rule, or the coke oven employee who is denied transfer to another department where it's easier to breathe, or the second helper on a basic oxygen furnace who is protesting an unjust incentive plan, away from the klieg lights of international union negotiations and testimonials, has been essentially omitted.

Little is mentioned or known of the activities and government of the 70,000 local unions in mills, mines, offices, factories, construction sites, stores, hospitals, railways, in which the members work under contracts and agreements they had little, if any, hand in negotiating. What about the local union officials and functionaries, presidents, secretaries, trustees, grievance committeemen, stewards, the overwhelming majority of whom work on the job in the plants along side the other members of the local union, and never met or saw Mr. George Meany or any other of the handful of Mr. Labors they read about or watch on television? What manner of men, or women, are these?

Local union leaders, when they are considered at all, are usually thought of as either ambitious apprentices or courtly sycophants awaiting their appointments to a desk in one of those office buildings where Mr. Labor has his desk, or, at the other extreme, they are the self-sacrificing visionaries, touched somewhere by Marx or Debs or Foster, for whom unions are a "cause", having to do with justice, rights, a change in the social system. (That the first category is growing, systematically encouraged and supported, and the second is dwindling, subtly curbed and restrained, are facts that must

*be weighed in speculating about the future of the labor move-
ment, as well as understanding the present.)*

*In viewing the leaders of local unions today, it is utter non-
sense to depend on these two extremes. More realistic and
down-to-earth considerations are more to the point.*

*(1) It is a way to "move up" in the COMPANY, to become
part of supervision. This ambition is fostered by the international union. In the steel union the pattern was charted in the
60's with the promotion of the union's research director, Har-
old Ruttenberg, to the position of vice-president of Ports-
mouth Steel Corporation. If the research director could
make it, what stood in the way of other loyal and dedicated
union officials? Such promotions (once considered "defections") to industry and government positions have been numerous on almost every level of the union, including the local
union. Local union officers and grievancemen swing into
management positions with the greatest of ease, provided
they have behaved themselves as union activists.*

*(2) It provides some extra loot—not big money—usually a
nominal salary ranging from five or ten dollars a month to
one hundred dollars a month, depending on the size of the local union, its financial strength, or the office or committee
post involved. There are relatively very few local unions in
the workplace that maintain full-time salaried officers or
grievancemen. Most local unions are small, under 1000 members, and can afford no more than nominal salaries for a fea-
sible number of officers and committeemen, in addition to the
payment of wages lost from work when it is required for union activity. Full-time salaries are more common in local
unions of the building and construction trades, and in exceptional factory or union situations, where dues is usually higher, and the full-time business agent's salary is the primary
expenditure of the local.*

*(3) A day off from the regular job, to perform "union busi-
ness" that is paid for by the local union treasury, can be a
welcome relief in the life of a worker. Such a day off for lo-*

*cal union functionaries is authorized when the officer or com-
mitteeman must attend a meeting or conference or to perform
any activity the union requests, during regular working
hours. It generally amounts to one or two days off a month,
sometimes more, depending on the functionary's responsibilities. (It can be, and sometimes is, abused.)*

*(4) A union officer's social life becomes expanded. It opens
up opportunities to travel to another city or to a downtown
hotel for some union function, or to attend a testimonial for a
big-shot labor leader, or politician. He is likely to be a delegate to a state labor convention at the capital city, or an international union convention in Las Vegas, Miami Beach, At-
lantic City or some other glamor spot. With some, it's a useful cover for a night out without bringing along the "old lady."*

*(5) Being part of an established and respected movement
that has a reputation for contributing to the welfare of the
workers, is a source of considerable social satisfaction and
fullfilment for many officers of local unions. Though it can't
be measured, and though workers who are attracted to activism in the union are, without doubt, already socially motivated, the active union member or officer reacts, noticeably, on a
higher level of social awareness and are much more respon-
sive to human concerns than the inactive members of the union.*

*(6) Local union officers are sometimes, though not as fre-
quently as is touted, chosen for salaried positions in the higher bodies of the labor movement. Applicants from universities, or, more often, the sons, brothers, in-laws, or nephews of
union leaders are moved into these positions, without regard
to the "eligible" local union functionaries.*

*(7) There is a place, usually precarious, in the local union,
for virile numbers of workers who are "oppositionists" pro-
pelled mainy by dreams of social change and the moral conviction that labor unions can be the vehicle to deliver this
change.*

James Lyons had lived the life of a blue collar worker long enough—actually he had never known any other life—that he was not a total stranger to the self-seeking motives that guided some of his brothers into union activities. There is no standard of weights and measures, no dip-stick to mark off the level of commitment to union principles, and, indeed, there is often so much conflict and confusion as to what these principles are, that he wasn't inclined to pass judgement on the moral and intellectual incentives that brought others into the same movement he had embraced. The bait dangled before the eyes of the self-seekers seemed to him a lot of rubbish, without real substance.

On the other hand he was often irked by the self-righteousness of the ideologues in the plant and union, who, somehow, never seemed to be around during the tedious and often hopeless complaints of workers who were in trouble with the company. Loftily, they preserved themselves for the more grandiose issues like the war in the Viet Nam, political moves in the White House, the conspiracy trial in Chicago or some other concern that seemed to him far removed from the mill or from their own lily-white departments. He felt that their virtue was irrelevant to the workplace, unreal, a lure, perhaps to snare esteem on the outside, an exotic toy to enjoy and show off. He realized he didn't understand what made them tick, and wasn't sure he lived on their planet.

As for himself, what was his angle? What made him tick? What did he hope to gain out of the union?

Though he had never taken an oath of poverty, he would, quite likely, vehemently condemn Jerry Rubin's sputtering remark, in *Growing Up at Thirty-Seven* that "Money for me is survival." Money had no such meaning for James Lyons. He had never given it such serious thought. He didn't come from a family with money and high living. He had never lived close to people with money, and didn't compete with them. He was a steady worker, and especially when he was on a six day work week, managed fairly well on his mill wages. He didn't gamble, didn't think of dealing, didn't dream of riches. None of his friends had more than he. In his own mind, those who held out on their union brothers to win favor with the company or recognition from the union officialdom, as he suspected some did, were the most contemptible creatures on the face of the earth.

Promotion in the company? Was he resigned to give this up? No, he wanted every promotion due him. He fought for the right of straddletruck operators to advance to locomotive engineers, a job closed to Blacks. But a management job, a turn foreman—never! He was well acquainted with the miserable lot of Black supervisors who were used as "Toms" and scapegoats, and lost their right to be a Black brother. To be a part of a management, that, without a pang of conscience, fired his friend Ben Chaney, was a thought that sickened him.

The honor and prestige of union leadership? Now, that was something different. Only a fanatic would consider this offensive. He understood well how union office gives one a different standing among workers, and that it is sometimes a slick cover for corruption, that it is looked upon as some sort of parasitic activity but the same can be said of almost any kind of leadership. Everyone should have pride in his own worth and how he puts it to use. Union office, like a judge's or deacon's should be properly respected. It should have dignity, status, beauty. Isn't that what he had sought at Bowen High School when he volunteered to play the role of Othello? Wasn't that the magic message his father gave him when they left Osceola for freedom in Chicago? It certainly was woven into his dreams about law school and defending victims of injustice. And it was the subtle strength in the Black handshake he gave a brother in the mill. He was ready.

Social change? Certainly. Of course. He didn't remember ever meeting a Black man opposed to social change. They come naturally to it, like businessmen come naturally to preservation. One needn't agree with the pronouncement that working men and working women "have nothing to lose but their chains," or, like Jack London, sign off their personal letters with "Yours for the Revolution" to know that all that ails the workers in the plant, or workers anywhere, white too, is that there isn't the least sense of equality between the owners of industry and those who do the productive work. *Social change*, the kind of change on the minds of the ten steelworkers who were killed at the plant gate in the Memorial Day parade of 1937, that was forged in bronze on the memorial plaque in front of the union hall, " ... *to promote industrial democracy and secure justice for workingmen and women everywhere* ... " even such a low-key goal, thirty five years later, was far off in the distance.

James, warily, rolled all these impressions and anxieties in his mind, and the idea of becoming a local union officer became more and more challenging. As a union officer he would be in a position to get the entire 4000 members behind the fight he seemed to be conducting single-handedly. On the other hand, it was because he wasn't "hooked up with that bunch (meaning the union leadership) who are always making excuses for the company" that many workers leaned towards him and made him their "unofficial grievanceman." Can one be "hooked up with that bunch" and, at the same time, be a rank and file leader?

James was elected, handily, with a vote that went far beyond the influence of the Black caucus, and he became the first Black secretary of Local 1033, United Steelworkers of America. (The international union, with a million and quarter members, had never, in all its history, had a Black secretary, or any Black member on its thirty-five man executive board.)

As the most recent addition to the local union's ruling body, and because he owed his election to the backing he received from the union's leadership (a reminder brandished day after day), and also because long union history decreed that a Black officer was to accept a subordinate place in asserting any authority or power, the new secretary, except for writing copious and dependable minutes of the meetings, felt disgruntled. He tried to steer the excutive board's deliberations towards the problems in the plant, but he couldn't succeed. The executive board was bogged down in a heap of red tape that had little to do with these problems. The Board saw its role as administrators, trustees, corporals for the international union, to rubber stamp its directives and follow its leadership. It was chiefly concerned with the inner problems of the union organizations, finances, union headquarters, sending delegates, approving resolutions, endorsing union sponsored candidates, support for proper community programs, educational classes, and on and on, but rarely about conditions in the workplace. Simply to administer the union and carry out the international union's policies and directives, weren't James' reasons for becoming a union officer. How many times he was instructed by the "experienced" officers that the union can't be bucking the company on everything, that the union has to go along, that collective bargaining was "give and take," and how many times he answered, innocently, as if he had memorized it in catechism, "the company represents only money; we represent the people!"

(The union contract provides for grievance committeemen in the various departments of the plant to handle the complaints of the workers on the job. But grievance committeemen are *not* officers of the union, and have no direct voice in setting policy for the union. Their jurisdiction, their activities, their rights to conduct union affairs are under the control of the union officers, and after the third step of a complex five-step grievance procedure, the elected grievance committeeman's jurisdiction is completely taken over by a staffman, appointed and salaried by the international union. This oligarchical procedure, depriving the workers of any meaningful control over their working conditions, with a number of illustrations from the workplace, is examined later in this volume.)

It wasn't in James' department, and as secretary of the local union it was not his problem. But he was involved with the Black caucus' inquiry into the Blast Furnace incentive plan. It was a lousy plan. An incentive plan is supposed to give workers an opportunity to increase their earnings by working faster and more efficiently. The way it works is that the company sets a certain production standard—so many tons per hour—which is one hundred per cent, and if production goes over that standard, the company and the workers share the increase on a fifty-fifty basis. One hundred and twenty per cent, and the workers on the crew would get an additional ten percent over their standard hourly wages. Sometimes production crews on furnaces or rolling mills would get incentive earnings amounting to thirty percent over their standard hourly rate. But the incentive plan in the Blast Furnace was set up so that "no matter how they busted their balls" they couldn't make more than two to three cents an hour—a dollar and a half to two dollars a pay. Because the blast furnace was a Black department, the workers believed their incentive plan was a racial problem, and that was the reason it became a matter for the Black caucus.

It was the last Tuesday of the month, the night for the regular monthly membership meeting of the local union, but for the workers in the blast furnace it was high noon, a showdown. A report was to be demanded at the meeting on the outcome of their grievance protesting their unfair incentive plan. Word spread that unless you were on the three to eleven shift, you better be at the meeting. They were there in mass, and tooks seats in the front row. The tension in the hall was such that the president, as he often did in such events, turned over the chair to the vice-president while he occupied himself with some papers. At the point of the meeting that a formal, routine report from the grievance chairman was being made, a blast furnace worker rose to his feet, and interrupted that the workers in the department wanted to know what was happening with their grievance. "You know, it's been three years since it was filed!" he shouted.

An exchange of glances from the chairman to the president to the international staffman, back to the chairman only made things worse. Were they hiding something?

A half dozen workers jumped to their feet. This wasn't simply a grievance that was being kicked about for three years. Many grievances were held up for longer periods. This grievance had become a symbol in many ways of racial descrimination, undemocratic procedures within the union, suppression of the rank and file, and company-union "deals." It had been signed by every last employee in the department. It had gone through every step of the grievance procedure, and was finally docketed for arbitration. But the rumor was that a pre-arbitration meeting had decided to withdraw the grievance, over the strong objections of the grievance committeeman, whose opinion carried no authority at that stage of the procedure.

It could no longer be kept a secret. The international staffman conceded that the blast furnace grievance had died a slow and lingering death. It was "withdrawn", because "it was technically defective" and it was "untimely," filed too late. (The contract says such grievances must be filed within a "reasonable" time after the installation of the incentive plan. What is "reasonable" in such cases has never been computerized.)

The meeting went up for grabs. Cries of "sell-out!" filled the meeting hall. Booing and hooting made it impossible to hear the angry questions and charges. The chair banged the gavel and threatened to clear the hall.

When quiet settled, James, seated on the platform, writing minutes, rose from his chair and said, "The men in the blast furnace have been robbed long enough. It's time to fight back. If the company refuses to settle this grievance on some technicality, we should all go downtown to the government, and file a complaint against the company." Again the meeting began to jump.

(Inviting or even hinting government intervention in a conflict between the company and the union is the ultimate in trade union apostasy. It is an unmistakable sign that the union has been invaded by a troublemaker, that a "cancer" was developing in the body of the union. This reaction is completely irrational, considering the clubby relationship between the international officers of the union and the officials in the U. S. Labor Department. The instances are indeed rare that a federal board—the NLRB, the LMRDA, the EECC—have ruled in favor of a rank and file worker who brought complaints against their union leaders. Local union leaders needlessly get upset about threats of their members to "go downtown." The LRMDA, established in 1959 under the provisions of the Landrum-Griffin bill, inaugurated "a bill of rights for union members." For ten years it had never made a ruling to overturn a single major union election. The massive complaints of the coal miners in the 1969 election of Tony Boyle over Jock Yablonski as president of the United Mine Workers of America was shunted aside by the LMRDA, emphatically ruling that the mine workers union election had been "conducted with the highest degree of honestly and integrity." It wasn't until the bullet-ridden bodies of Yablonski and his wife and daughter were found, that the LMRDA and the United States Department of Labor conceded there was wrong-doing, and ordered a new election.)

The meeting adjourned in confusion, and the executive board called its members together for an emergency meeting. There, James was scolded, questioned, advised, and warned about disruptive activities.

The following day James was informed by the local president that he couldn't take off the one day a month for union business to attend to some of his official duties, because "there was a shortage of funds."

In rapid succession he was disciplined by the company with a one day suspension, then a three day suspension, followed by a five day suspension for alleged infractions of company rules. These included "doing union business on company time." "being away from his own work area," and "failure to observe safety rule Number Six."

He knew the meaning of that pattern. It was a warning the company was out to fire him. Of course, he couldn't be handled as callously as was his friend Ben Chaney. He had more seniority. He had a reputation as a reliable worker. He had a popular following in the plant. He wasn't a "hard core" worker, under a yellow-dog contract. The union had no choice but to stand up for him. The reaction of the Black caucus and other rank and file people had to be reckoned with.

When James told the local union executive board about the company's harassment, some were sympathetic, but the final word was, "You better straighten out."

He learned how to travel that dangerously desperate road that was barricaded at one end by a obsequious union leadership that was caught up in a rickety system of collective bargaining, and on the other end by a company management that had not fully emerged from its pre-union days of Tom Girdler and the Memorial Day massacre.

James' term as local union secretary lasted just long enough to conserve him for the rank and file movement in the plant. He was not re-elected as secretary, out-foxed by an election maneuver that pitted two Blacks against a single white candidate, and victimized by a barrage of McCarthyism.

Every summer, during his vacation, he returns to Osceola, Arkansas, to enjoy the muddy river full of catfish, the generous countryside alive with rabbits and pheasant, and his old family friends who want to hear his success story in Chicago. He tells them that someday it's got to get better for working people, and that someday he's going to straighten out Republic Steel.

Inside Collective Bargaining

Chapter Seven

Union Headquarters is Far
from the Workplace

Except for a narrowing "lunatic fringe" of the business community which claims that labor unions are a communist conspiracy, and a yet-narrower group of far-out Marxists who claim labor unions are the chief obstacles to workers' revolution, there is surprisingly meager criticism or examination of the institution of *collective bargaining* anywhere in the United States. Workers, bosses, corporate executives, stock-holders, banks, churches, Congress, the courts, just about everybody—including, even, employers and universities that have been successful in preventing outside unions from organizing their workers—consider collective bargaining to be a patriotic, if not divine, institution. The words themselves sound so right and clean. They have the flavor of fairness and balance.

Collective bargaining is a broad and complex relationship of mutuality, cooperation and trust between organized labor, industry and government. It is established by law, and its agreements and procedures are enforceable in the courts. It is an all-inclusive term that is considered to be synonymous with peaceful partnership between Labor and Capital, fair wages and decent working conditions, even-handed procedures for

handling workers' complaints, proper recognition of managements' rights, efficient machinery for restricting and disciplining workers in the plants, and, it is claimed to have all but obliterated class antagonisms in the United States.

But, viewed from inside the workplace, the catchy claims
made for collective bargaining, have a hard time taking hold.
For instance, blue collar workers don't consider themselves
equal partners with management, and they have a great deal
of trouble with many other touted benefits of the collective
bargaining process. Those who actually work under collective
bargaining agreements would like fundamentally to change its
rules. Stripped of its fripperies, collective bargaining is what
goes on between the top officers of international unions and
industry when they join in negotiations for a new labor contract which fixes wages, pensions, grievance procedure, holi-
days, vacations, unemployment benefits, seniority rights for
the employees of an industry or corporation. It is an elaborate,
preciously private ceremony, diligently kept out of view of the
workers whose affairs are being decided. Even after a contract
has been agreed upon, this disposition for smartness and se-
crecy persists, and its provisions are announced piece-meal,
grudgingly, as if it were nobody's business but the negotiators'. There is a lapse of months, sometimes a year, before a
printed contract is passed out to the members of the union,
while management people and union staff have xeroxed copies
which they keep close to their chests. After it is too late, workers may discover questionable provisions in their new contract.

(A challenge in the federal court in Pittsburgh, Pennsylvania, by a small group of rank and file steelworkers, in 1974,
that a surprise contract provision for binding arbitration together with a no-strike clause, was in violation of union members' rights, was denied by Judge Hubert Teitlebaum. The
judge was convinced when he asked the international union
president why this new provision, called the Experimental Negotiating Agreement, hadn't been discussed beforehand with

the union members or in the columns of its monthly journal, and president I.W. Abel answered that "it might have been rejected had it received advanced publicity." The same reasoning was offered by a witness for the federal government, William J. Usery, Jr., then the director of the federal Mediation and Conciliation Service. He testified that "membership involvement would decrease the possibility of the agreement." Mr. Usery explained his interest in the suit was that the no-strike and binding arbitration agreement would eliminate "crisis bargaining" and that it was vital to the economy of the country. A year later, he was appointed by President Ford to become Secretary of Labor, and he received a message from Mr. Abel that "the recognition offered you at this time is well-earned.")

The International Union headquarters, and the corporate boards are far from the mills, shops, yards and factories where the collective bargaining agreements are enforced.

It's what goes on *after* the contract has been signed, *after* the parties have leaned over the bargaining table to shake hands while the news-cameras click, *after* the parties have returned to their respective offices and headquarters for a final huddle to explain to their boards what they had signed, when the principals are no longer the highly glamorized presidents and vice-presidents of the International Union and the Corporation, but are, instead, the sweaty blue collar workers and the lower management people in the workplace, that the *real* problems of collective bargaining are revealed.

In modern times, it is the rule for a single labor agreement to cover the workers of an entire industry, involving a number of corporations and dozens of industrial plants in the United States and Canada, as, for example, the steel industry. In auto, electrical manufacturing, farm equipment, rubber, textiles, coal mining, teamsters and all mass production industries, the practice is substantially the same. The pattern adopted in 1974 by the Phelps-Dodge Mining Corporation, and by the Dow-Chemical, to name a few, where coalitions of several competing unions in the corporation's plants were established at the insistence of the corporations to negotiate a single contract, has emerged as a standardized rule in collective bargaining.

Protestations against industry-wide bargaining, once a popular plank in the platforms of right-wing groups, aren't taken seriously any more. It's clear the corporations would not have it any other way, the government has encouraged it, and for the international union leaders it has been a blessing.

But such blanket labor contracts, dealing with the broad issues of the industry, give scant attention to the every day working conditions in the various workplaces, and leave the local unions and their memberships out in the cold, without power to confront local management. To most union members it is the local issues that are the most real. The national issue of wages, are felt to be beyond their control, dictated, they suspect, by the government. Pensions? Cost of living increments? Safety and Health? That's decided in Washington, or Pittsburgh, or Detroit, not by the workers in the plant. But a three-day suspension for punching in late, a denial of a promotion when it was due, cheating employees on their incentive earnings? Those are the issues that must be settled in the workplace, and they have to be settled under the evasive, and often contradictory, terms of, and in the manner prescribed by, the labor contract which they had no hand in negotiating.

In the zero hour of the 1976 New York City transport workers negotiations, union officials who were members of the bargaining committee, were, in their own words, "outside, twiddling our thumbs," while the *real* power, the government and the industry, was settling the terms of the contract, incidentally, without any provision for a wage increase. In the Chicago Teachers Union negotiations in 1975, the city mayor took over from the union and the board of education, and set the terms of the contract. In the strange teamsters union negotiations of 1976, the wantonly ill-timed threat of a Taft-Hartley injunction by the new U. S. Labor secretary, while both parties were in session, emphasized the serious symptoms of decay in the collective bargaining system.

The members of the union who are in the workplace every day are far removed from the rites and rituals of labor relations and the collective bargaining process, and, except when a strike is called, seldom are permitted a role. Their's is but to comply and applaud. Local union committees and grievance-men in the workplace, with rare exceptions, do not engage in collective bargaining, as is commonly thought. This is a willfully disseminated myth. In many unionized workplaces there are no local committees or persons authorized to handle workers' complaints. The international union or its paid representatives, who are not employed in the workplace, handle the workers' complaints or contract violations. And where such local committees and grievance procedure are part of the union structure, the power of the local union committees to act is extremely restricted. They are empowered to do no more than attempt to persuade the plant management to carry out the agreements signed by their international officers. And if the plant management has a conflicting interpretation of the meaning of these agreements, the local union may file a grievance. The grievance is ultimately settled outside the workplace, by the international union's staffman and the corporation's industrial relations counsellor, often a year or more after the grievance had been filed, or by an arbitrator after a three year wait.

The pioneers and apostles of the collective bargaining process can and do advance forceful argument that it is "the living end" of labor-management co-existence, that it is the highest expression of industrial democracy for the workers, that the signed contracts are a faithful expression of the workers' demands, negotiated by international officers and bargaining committees elected by the workers.

In the workplace the reaction of the employees to the contract settlements produced by their international officers is seldom that profuse or generous. It generally runs a narrow range from the cynical "we were sold down the river," to the resentful "it was rammed down our throats," to the shrug that translates into "what can we do? It's better than a strike." Even the local union officers avoid defending the contract if they plan to run for re-election. Only the international union's staff give it unstinted praise.

As a rule, in those unions in which members have secured the formal right to vote on a new labor contract, the terms of the contract are not known to the members until they have been publicly announced in the news media. By then the previous contract has already expired as of that midnight, and the union members are still at work, before they have had a chance to vote for or against the newly signed contract. Or, if they had been on strike, the consequences of a vote to reject the contract are staggering. There's no estimating how long it could take a repudiated and smarting leadership to negotiate a better contract. It's a "yes" or "no" vote, and amounts to a vote of confidence or no confidence in the international union. The vote, often involving local union memberships of as many as 20,000, (most locals have fewer than a thousand members) is hastily ordered and arranged. Little or no time is provided for a discussion or briefing on the new contract, which the members know only from the announcements in the media. The international staffman, or the local union president, has a copy of the *highlights* of the new contract which they haven't had a chance to study, and they honestly plead ignorance on the specifics of the new contract. The full weight of the international union bears down on the membership for an after-the-fact approval. In those relatively rare instances that the membership has rejected a newly negotiated labor agreement, the most extreme fury of the international union, the industry and the government, threatening the direst consequences, has usually been enough to restore the membership to its senses. A most unparliamentary "re-vote" was ordered by UAW president Walter Reuther when the membership rejected a GM contract the union had negotiated.

Among the large international unions, next to the UAW, the United Steelworkers of America (USWA) is considered, at least by the public, as one of the more democratically administered unions in the United States. Yet USWA, from its earliest beginning has rejected every move for the right of the membership to vote on union contracts.

As early as 1937, Philip Murray, the sainted labor leader and first president of the steelworkers union, explained to the union's first Wage and Policy Convention that contract negotiations had to be tightly controlled, without direct involvement of the elected delegates, or of the rank and file steelworkers.

"I invite your views on the wage-policy question," said Murray, "but recommend that the matter of negotiating a satisfactory wage agreement to succeed the one which will expire on February 28, 1938, be left entirely in the hands of the Executive Officers and the scale committee (appointed) . . . .We are mindful of the fact that our organization has been built so rapidly in the past 18 months that there has not been sufficient opportunity for the development of leadership in our own ranks . . . " (None of the Executive Officers or members of the scale committee were steelworkers.)

At the second Wage and Policy Convention in 1940, it soon became apparent that the steelworkers still suffered from under-development, and the convention adopted a resolution authorizing "the international officers to exercise their best judgement in promoting improvements in the present wage structure . . . " Again, no workers are involved.

On and on it continued, and in 1950, at the fifth Constitutional Convention of the steelworkers, Philip Murray, relying less on his venerable image (somewhat tarnished by his purge of dissidents in the union) than upon his almost absolute organizational control of the convention delegations, called upon the convention to vote down a resolution requesting membership ratification of labor agreements. "We don't do as a lot of organizations do . . . .with respect to the collective bargaining process. The policy of the Steelworkers Union . . . is the policy of the United Mineworkers Union . . . I happen to be one of those who assisted that organization's policy for . . . 28 or 30 years, and the mineworkers union never raised objections to this policy because they found out in the end that they were able to get more out of it." (It was the "model" United Mineworkers that was for years the center of the stormiest battles in labor union history, centered, principally, around the very issue of the miner's right to "raise objections." This internal conflict culminated in the hideous assassination of the union's opposition leader, Jock Yablonski, and his wife and daughter, for which the international president and several of his aides were convicted in early 1974.)

After the death of Philip Murray, his successors, first David J. MacDonald, later I. W. Abel, managed to head off all efforts of the union membership to permit ratification of the labor agreement. By their shrewd control of convention delegates, one third of whom have always been staffmen not employed in the industry, and the skillful manipulation of the democratic process at the convention, the proponents of membership ratification always found themselves in a helpless minority.

As in diplomacy between nations, when secret agreements remained secret for many years, coming to the surface only under circumstances of political change, in collective bargaining too, there are tacit understandings and unspoken agreements between the international union and the corporation that have taken years to uncover.

A classic example was the experience in the basic steel industry where Black steelworkers were systematically blocked from transferring into departments traditionally filled with white steelworkers, in spite of the seniority provisions of the union contract which was amended in 1965 to conform legally with the Civil Rights Act. But it wasn't until a federal court ruling in 1974, which, in response to a suit by the NAACP against the steel corporations and the international union (there were a number of successful court actions under Title VII of the Civil Rights Act involving several corporations and unions) ordered the companies and the union to halt the violations of Black workers' seniority rights, that both parties to the labor agreement permitted the transfer of Blacks to "white" departments. The union contract did not require a single word to be changed to accomplish this change in policy. It was in the contract all the time—in fuzzy language, but it was there. Unenforced, inoperative. Many scores of grievances in behalf of Black workers seeking to transfer to other departments where it was better were filed by local grievancemen, but not one of these grievances reached arbitration. *In all unionized industry, according to the Labor Law Journal, up until 1973, only thirty-five union grievances charging racial discrimination were reported as reaching arbitration.*

Similarly, a pattern of tacit agreement between corporate and international unions providing for the discharge of employees because of wage garnishments, or police records, or lack of a high school diploma, continued for as long as the federal courts remained silent. Local unions grievances protesting these policies as discriminatory against Blacks never got far in the grievance procedure. The international union refused to process them in the higher steps. The turn-over in employment of Blacks in the mills, until recently, reached more than eighty per cent—most of them fired for arbitrary and unrelated breaches of factory rules.

When collective bargaining between the corporations and the union shifts from the relaxed hotels and offices in Washington, New York, or Pittsburgh, to the tense, dehumanized factories, mills, and shops, where the blue collar worker daily comes face to face with the nuts and bolts of the labor agreement, one experiences a startling transformation of collective bargaining. There the entire process has been restructured, with tight restrictions and precise rules, and a totally different style, registering the fundamental inequality of the bargaining parties. In the workplace, the union representative is an *employee* of the *company* (not of the union) and, of course, so is the person who has filed a complaint or grievance. On the other side of the bargaining table is the *boss* (the guy who can make life miserable for an employee). The boss has an advantage in bargaining, which, when push comes to shove, the company can and does use with predictable effect. Industrial relations people on the plant level regularly remind local union people that there is no collective bargaining in the plant—that they do no more than carry out the provisions of the labor agreement and try to get the employees to do the same. If there is any serious disagreement between the local union and the company about the interpretation of the labor agreement, this is resolved somewhere other than in the plant. Contract disputes are settled, ultimately, in an involved process, between the international union and the corporation.

Scholars, government agencies, international union journals, the media and the labor movement itself give very little notice to labor-management affairs in the workplace. As far as they are concerned, the conflict had ended when the parties attached their signatures to the labor agreement, and will stand undisturbed, until the next contract negotiations take place in three or four years.

But that's not the way it is. Every day, in almost every workplace, workers file countless complaints and grievances, (if there is a procedure for doing so) claiming the company is being unfair and in violation of the contract. On ocassion, an outbreak such as at the G.M. plant at Lordstown, Ohio, may create panic or celebration (depending on one's political leanings) and might create some doubts about the omnipotence of the collective bargaining system. For many, it was the first they had heard that there were 16,000 grievances filed by the employees in that one single Vega plant, all of them unheard, unsettled, collapsed, buried in paper procedures, not negotiated—contrary to what the labor agreement specified. Such "collective bargaining" activities never hit the headlines. In every workplace in the United States there is a comparable

yearly collapse in the settling of grievances. (At the Republic
Steel plant in South Chicago an average of five hundred
grievances that are signed by more than twenty-five hundred
workers, one half the entire work-force, are filed each year.
Of course, they don't get settled. They are denied the benefits
of collective bargaining.

There's hardly a pretense at subtlety. The downright blunt
techniques of *not* settling grievances, *not* observing the contract, *not* bargaining on working conditions, not even going
through the motions of the grievance procedure in the workplace tells more about labor-management relations than the
highly-publicized, extravagantly praised, flavorous contract
talks between the corporation and international union leaders.

It is this unrecorded, unnoticed, part of the collective bargaining process that we are undertaking to fill in here. It's the
brass tacks of the system. It's the part that most pragmatically affects the blue collar worker.

The principle elements in the high record of failure of
collective bargaining in the workplace are (1) the outrageous
inequality of the two parties, (2) the hardening anti-union
posture of corporate industry in periods of economic uncer-
tainty and social imbalance, (3) the phenomenal successes of
highly-centralized union bureaucracies, bolstered by the
State, in reducing the self-government and bargaining power
of the local union in the workplace, and (4) the systematic dis-
engagement of collective bargaining and grievance machinery
so that it doesn't function at the "lower levels" of labor-management relationships.

Blue collar workers, (and white collar workers, too) who
have experienced the controls and restraints of their union
contracts and their international union staff, are made aware
every day that the "equal partnership" of collective bargaining doesn't apply in the workplace, and as soon as they come
in conflict with the boss, learn that *International Union Headquarters is Far from the Workplace*.

The inequality we are treating here is not of an abstract or moralistic nature, nor an appeal for esteem. Because it is commonly assumed that LABOR is George Meany, Leonard Woodcock, Frank Fitzsimmons, Jerry Wurf, Robert Georgine or other international union figures being seen coming in and out of the White House, or mingling freely with leaders of business and government, it doesn't seem to register that it is altogether different in the workplace. In the workplace, the people who speak for Labor and represent the workers in any dispute with the company aren't important public figures. They are people who punch a time-clock every day as employees of the same management whose workers they represent, and this one factor is a near-fatal limitation to free, unhindered, uncoerced, collective bargaining. How is this different, for instance, from a Congressman's salary paid directly by Exxon, or an alderman's salary paid monthly by a steel company? Who would ever expect such a congressman or alderman properly to represent their constituents? In many unions, even the time taken from work by the local union official is paid by the employer. It is provided for under some labor contracts, and was much more widespread during World War II, when union-management accord was considered the key to victory over Fascism. But, of course, the local union activist's posititon isn't the same as a congressman on the payroll of the oil company. The comparison is suggested here only to focus on this one particular snag in the collective bargaining system in the workplace.

Company management, when pressed, when accused of violating the union contract, when charged with favoritism, isn't likely to allow the worker on the other side of the bargaining table to forget his status as a worker for the company. No local union committeeman, no matter how constant and faithful to principle, can afford to be lighthearted toward his own vulnerability in the workplace. Quite innocently, one can get into all sorts of trouble on a blue collar job—enough to be fired. Infractions of work rules that might be overlooked in some cases, can, when committed by a local union activist, become a federal offense. Most union stewards in the workplace, (how does one honor the precious exceptions?) aren't prepared to get bloodied in a battle with the company. Especially where the local union has been shorn of any effective power to fight back.

The very structure of the workplace, the discipline and rules, the chain of command, the pressures of competition, the intimidating working conditions of the employees, balanced on the edge of hard times, scheduled for a lay-off or short work weeks, their raw exposure to unsafe and unhealthful practices, the hassle in reporting off for illness or personal business, the anti-labor orientation of lower-level supervision, and so very, very, many autocratic subtleties, all distinctly taint the wells of industrial demorcracy and good-faith bargaining. The confirmed hierarchy of the modern industrial plant demolishes any egalitarian notions of workers and bossess as partners in industry. No, not even if the worker is an elected union spokesman, a local union president or grievanceman, no, not as long as he or she is at the same time an employee of the company.

Though all labor agreements between industry and unions contain, in very general language, a provision which recognizes the role of local union officers, grievanceman or stewards in the workplace, (recognized also by federal labor law) the agreements spell out, in the most unequivocal language those union activities which are *forbidden* in the workplace. Strictly forbidden are "union activities on company time" or union activities "in any manner which shall interfere with production."

Innocent enough if the words are read in a seminary, but in the workplace they are a trap! A legitimate complaint about an unsafe condition on the job, as, for instance, the scarfing of leaded steel, can be, and has been, interpreted as "interfering with production," and the worker who complains with any persistence, can be, and has been disciplined. A grievanceman listening to a worker's urgent complaint about a contract violation, or who talks to another worker about a personal matter, can be nailed for "performing union business on company time." How forcefully the company may pursue such ingenious accusations depends upon the union-management climate in the plant. If it's gentle, reliable and accomodating, the company doesn't bother and may even show its appreciation. If there is a climate of "unreasonableness" or the union committeeman "has a bug up his ass," watch out! Federal law and contracts have rarely been adequate to protect such a committeeman or local union officer from becoming a victim. Disciplinary suspensions and discharge from employment for causes that are manifestly suspect continue to play an important role in management's collective bargaining posture in the plant. An influential and frequently-quoted labor arbitrator, in ruling against a steelworkers union activist who was disciplined for protesting a working condition, proclaimed that "a steel mill is not a debating society," and those words have had the impact of the Sermon on the Mount inside the workplaces of America. *Don't argue with the boss!*

Local unions are losing, if they have not already lost, their basic function in the workplace (unless that function is seen, as it is by industry and some critics who have given up on the labor movement, as one to keep the worker in line). They are not taken very seriously by the management, and it is often confident that the international union is in its corner. The local unions are losing, if they have not already lost, their primary role as the basic component of orgainzed labor. The dues-payers, the fighting troops, the rank and file, without whom, it would seem, there is no labor movement, have little to say in running the affairs of their union or exerting their influence in the workplace.

The rights and initiatives of the local union in the workplace have been methodically gagged and undone.

First, the international union deprived the local unions of all rights to a voice in determining wages or other financial benefits for their members. The international union, in most negotiations, decides these matters, and the local union, for the most part, is kept in complete ignorance about what is being bargained for. They know only what the media leaks to the public, and they learn of the settlement in the same manner. The majority of union members have no right, and, where they have the formal right, no real opportunity to approve or disapprove the contract negotiated by their international union. Whatever pressures are felt by the international officers are not from the local unions, as such, but, more often, from dissident rank and file groups within the local unions. Local union presidents and officers rarely affiliate openly with dissident groups, and generally try to rush in and be the first to hail the new contract as the greatest in history, to get their brownie points from the international officials.

Secondly, the international union deprived the local union of what has always been recognized as its main source of power—*the right to strike.* (The exceptions which the international unions cite to detract from this charge are hardly worth taking seriously.) A strike called by a local union without the sanction of the international union is denounced as a "wildcat," and local union leaders who become involved in a "wildcat" inevitably risk the fall of a two-edged ax. While the company sharpens one side, the international union sharpens the other. Heads roll. The company, under the terms of the contract, distributes discharge notices. The international union. under the terms of the union constitution, removes elected members from their local union offices.

Third, the financial affairs of a local union are subject to the absolute control of the international union. The local union no longer even collects the dues of the union members. The company checks off the dues from the workers' pay, and sends it, no, not to the local union, but to the international union. The local union is returned a fixed portion of the dues, usually less than half, but the international union may, if it deems a union has stepped out of line, completely withold the locals' share, and completely deprive it of its treasury.

Fourth, local union officers and grievancemen may be suspended or removed from their elected positions by the international officers, and the affairs of the local union placed under the control of the international union. This right is somewhat limited by the Landrum-Griffin law, but it is not prohibited, and it rarely stands in the way or supports any membership protest against the establishment of a trusteeship over a local union. The membership of the local union has absolutely no voice in the naming of trustees.

Fifth, the grievance procedure in the workplace is an inequitable, treacherous and maddening system, willfully drawn to give management a strong upper hand—a broad and sweeping concession to the corporations' persistent demand, written into all labor agreements, in almost identical language, that *"The Company retains the exclusive rights to manage the business and plants and to direct the working forces."* (Quoted from Article Fifteen of the steel industry labor agreement.) The procedure obstructs more than it eases the highly-vaunted, free, democratic approach to worker-management disputes. Woven into the procedure is a fussily rigid and unworkable calendar of deadlines that succeeds in dispatching an endless number of written and signed grievances of workers to that trash-heap stamped *"untimely"*, not discussable, to be carted away by the janitorial staff in the office of industrial relations. The procedure grants the company numerous other exemptions and advantages. In some categories of readily-acknowledged violations, where the boss will tell the protesting worker, "my hands are tied, go ahead and file a grievance, but do as you're told," it is profitable for the company *not* to bargain, to procrastinate, to stonewall until it is ready to return to the provisions of the contract. Indeed, if Moses had been subject to the procedures of the modern union contract, he never could have negotiated so successfully with God. An article in *Steel Labor* (August 1974), official journal of the international union in steel, reported that Wayne Anderson, vice-president of the Pittron Foundry in Glassport, Pennsylvania, was exploring an innovative approach to the grievance procedure in his plant. "At every meeting with the union," he told the journal reporter, "there's an extra chair. It's there for Jesus Christ, Whom I ask to sit and give His guidance, wisdom and understanding." To what degree this made the grievance procedure more workable wasn't reported in *Steel Labor.*

Barring a miracle, unless a powerful democratic movement among rank and file workers develops, collective bargaining will continue to head in the direction of tighter and tighter controls in the hands of the top union leadership, with greater and greater restrictions on the rights of members to decide on their labor agreements or to call a strike in their workplace, more ambiguities and complexities to frustrate any challenge to management in the plants, greater intervention by the State on the side of employers, with more frequent use of court injunctions against unions to enforce industrial peace.

The union must be brought into the workplace, so a worker with a complaint, or a beef, or a grievance, could get it settled. That's the first and most basic step.

Chapter Eight

Five Steps to Failure

It's probably a safe bet that most Americans, including unionized workers, have never read or even fingered a collective bargaining agreement, and aren't really familiar with the grievance procedures that collective bargaining has established in the workplaces. Since it is the principal statement of this book that "the proper study of the blue collar worker is the workplace," and because the grievance procedure has become the single most important social mechanism for recording the blue collar workers' resistance to "lousy" working conditions, the reader is entitled to more than the shallow boasts of partisans that the workers have found in the grievance procedure a decent and dependable technique for protecting themselves against all possible employer encroachments. The reader is also, of course, entitled to more than a bitter attack on the system as a "sell-out", although by now evidence is piling up that the grievance procedure in the workplace is not the highest expression of peoples' struggle for industrial democracy.

A step-by-step description of the grievance procedure, exactly as happens in the workplace, is essential at this point in our examination.

The grievance procedure is constructed like a pyramid, with five ascending steps. Five steps may not seem monumental. But as one views it in perspective, *Step Five* is miles, and years, and worlds distant from *Step One.*

Step One is an informal, spontaneous, person-to-person exchange between the worker and the department supervisor or foreman in which the worker claims the company had violated the union agreement. In more familiar terms, it might be compared to a situation where a motorist, ticketed by a traffic cop for allegedly speeding, insists the speedometer registered exactly thirty-five miles an hour, but the cop is firm and doesn't back off. The motorist can elect either to pay the twenty-five dollar fine, without going to court, or stand trial in court. In similar manner, a worker who believes the boss is compelling him, in violation of the union contract, to perform certain duties, may, if the boss is firm and doesn't back off, elect to do as he's ordered, or file a union grievance appealing the boss' decision. The first complaint is *Step One*, the appeal is to *Step Two*, just as the cop's ticket is step one and the appeal to traffic court is step two. However, there is an important difference.

In the traffic court there's a judge of a sort, either elected or appointed, probably a political hack, and possibly not above accepting a bribe, but regardless of these flaws, the judge is not a cop out of the same precinct as the cop who issued the ticket. That, anyone would agree, would give the appeal all the appearance of a bum rap. On the other hand, when we look at *Step Two* of the grievance procedure in the plant, who do we find in charge? We find another company boss, usually the superintendent or the assistant superintendent, who, in the first place had undoubtedly ordered the foreman to have the worker perform the duties which are being protested. Otherwise the foreman would have backed off before the grievance was appealed to *Step Two*. Foremen frequently admit they have their orders from the superintendent and their hands are tied. The same superintendent, without as much as covering his business suit with a black robe, becomes the judge in *Step Two,* and makes the decision either to uphold his foreman or to decide in favor of the complaining worker, who in *Step Two* has his union grievanceman representing him. Consider, too, that the superintendent has another contaminating connection to *Step Two.* Both the worker and the union grievanceman have their wages paid by the superintendent, or by the company, and that can become pretty sticky. From then on, any likening of *Step Two* with any known juridical system or due process of law would be far-fetched.

If the superintendent agreed with the union, and ruled against his own foreman and in favor of the aggrieved worker, that would end the grievance—*settled in Step Two*—and the working condition grieved against would be eliminated. But, except in a piddling matter, that's a rare, an extremely rare, disposition of a worker's grievance. More than nine out of ten grievances appealed to *Step Two* are denied by the superintendents, on the basis of Article Fifteen of the union contract, that "the Company retains the exclusive rights to manage the business and plants, and to direct the working forces." Such a management clause is written into practically every union-management agreement, and it is the cornerstone of company discipline. There is no pretense that the labor-management "partnership" evolved in collective bargaining has in any manner diminished "management's right to manage."

(In an interesting analysis of a typical union contract, Mike Holodnak, a teacher of Labor at Bridgeport (Conn.) University, listed fourteen "rights", of which five are management rights, eight are "joint" rights, and only one is a union-right—the right to elect union stewards. But the "right of management to manage" reduces all other rights in the workplace to meaningless babble.)

The union, confronted with the superintendent's rejection of the grievance in *Step Two,* must decide either to drop the grievance, or to appeal it to the next higher step, *Step Three.*

Many factors must be considered by the union, other than the merit of the grievance. The international union is yelling that the grievancemen are appealing too many grievances, "for political reasons." There are already five or six hundred grievances in the plant waiting to be heard in *Step Three*. (In the GM plant in Lordstown, Ohio there were twenty thousand grievances waiting to be heard.) The superintendent is delivering hints of "cracking down" in the department against "poor production records" and high levels of "absenteeism" all meant to intimidate, to discourage union muscle.

To get along with the procedure, let us assume the grievance is appealed to *Step Three*. What happens in that step of the grievance procedure? In a plant the size, and with the problems of Republic Steel in South Chicago, the appeal is listed at the bottom of the heap, and it would be normal to take a year or two for the grievance to reach the *Third Step* agenda, for a hearing.

In Step Three, the grievance becomes more depersonalized. The aggrieved worker and the boss have been eased out of it. It has become a matter between the company's industrial relations officers and the chairman of the union's grievance committee.

Industrial relations departments are not, as they are sometimes alleged to be, impartial peoples' advocates, devoted to high principles of collective bargaining and benevolence in the workplace, a wall of protection between the hot, unyielding tempers of Workers and Bosses. Such illusions are frequently fostered in the workplace and elsewhere, and it should not have to be said, because it is self-evident, that the industrial relations departments are part of the hierarchy of plant management, with a specialized role to provide legal, moral and popular support for the company's operational and labor policies. Industrial relations counsellors are somewhat like chaplains in the armed forces, given officer's rank, but without any command or any real participation in the business of the military; or similar to the intellectual at the international union headquarters who prepares the speeches and reports for the officers but are not privvy to their understandings with the corporations. Industrial relations people come to *Step Three* with attache cases filled with past arbitration decisions, grievance settlements that bear the union's signature, copies of local agreements agreed to by the union, and a dossier on the aggrieved worker, all lined up to sustain the company's position. What new weapon does the union representative have to beat down the company's massive defenses? Nothing that wasn't previously demonstrated in Steps One and Two. The facts in the grievance don't change. The language of the contract doesn't change. History is on the side of the company, in that its actions will certainly be upheld, and the workers' grievance, in ninety per cent of the cases, will be side-tracked. Any worker who has been around for a while can testify to the accuracy of that observation.

At this point, the union has to make a decision whether the year already spent on this grievance is worth the trouble. It would take another six months to a year before it could be heard in *Step Four* provided the staffman of the international union agreed to have it heard in that step.

The international union staff representative servicing a local union turns down most grievances seeking a hearing in *Step Four,* usually on the grounds the grievance doesn't have sufficient merit, and often for strategic reasons unexplained to either the worker or the local union. The staffman's decision on this matter is final. But, assuming in this case, that the decision is to go through with a fourth step hearing, what new definitions or elements of justice are anticipated here?

Under the procedure, *Step Four* is a hearing between the company's industrial relations superintendent together with a corporation attorney on one side, and the international union's staffman on the other. Do they know something the local union people or the plant industrial relations counselors don't know? Is there a new set of finger prints or a surprise witness waiting to be introduced? Nothing. Nothing new, except that the people making the decision are now one more step removed from the workplace.

The international union staffman is a paid employee of the international union ($25000 a year plus expenses, and more in some unions) and is not an employee of the company. Though he, neither, is taken into confidence in the tacit agreements worked out between the corporation and the international union during contract negotiations, he is astute enough to understand that there is a "good," a "civilized," an arm-in-arm relationship between the international union officers and the corporation heads, and that "rocking the boat" isn't appreciated by the international executive board. Of course, the members of the union in the workplace, though they don't elect the union staffmen, can raise a storm. But they can't dismiss him, and sometimes a bit of a conflict with the members even gives the staffman a better image with the international. He is taught early in his career as a staffman never to allow the members to push him.

Industrial relations, in *Step Four,* is confident that it can hold to its orginal contentions if that's what the company wants. There is prudent concern on its part that the grievance procedure continue to maintain an unblemished reputation, and that workers aren't led to the conclusion that there is no hope in the grievance procedure for settling the workers complaints. Too stubborn a stand against workers' grievances risks the build-up of frustration among the workers, a loss of confidence in the union, "wildcat" strikes, or other extreme expressions of workers' resistance, which can, in the long run, be harmful to the corporation. Skilled industrial relations people are supposed to be hypersensitive to such developments.

But otherwise it is all to the company's advantage to mark time, to be unyielding, to stonewall. Delay is in the company's favor. It can't interfere with production. The company isn't hurting. Management's position remains in full force during all the steps of the grievance procedure, and even if, at some point, the company were to relent, it often would have achieved most of its purposes during the long period of grievance discussion and appeals, and often the remedy sought by the union would have become moot, no longer having practical application. The company gambles in *Step Four,* knowing all the cards the union holds. The union's only bluff is *Step Five—arbitration.* Of the hundreds of grievances filed by each local union, how many can possibly be arbitrated in a year? The Company knows precisely how many.

There is a widespread impression that in a plant where arbitration is provided for in the union contract, that, ultimately, all disputes are settled by an arbitrator, to the satisfaction of all concerned parties, and that arbitration is truly the summit where peace, justice and industrial democracy reign supreme.

A closer look at the workplace shows that arbitration—the final step in the pyramid of grievance procedure—has failed to satisfy the worker or to fullfil the union's promise of a fair and equitable system for settling their disputes with the management.

Strangely, labor arbitration has escaped critical study and for more than a quarter of a century has enjoyed a mystical and splendorous status, greater, in many respects, to that of the CIA, the Puritan Ethic, St. Anne's Shrine, or the United States Census. Opinion on labor arbitration shows no appreciable division, no subtle distinctions between left and right, no labor-capital conflict, no generational dispute. It's about unanimous. Inseparable from the collective bargaining system, no institution in the United States is more firmly entrenched.

What qualifications do labor arbitrators have to make judgements on the grievances in the workplace? (We shall have an opportunity to observe them in action in the case histories of later chapters in this book.) They are mostly an anonymous lot, except for a small handful of annointed "authorities." They have spent their adult lives in lusterless careers as lawyers, and few, if any, have any background in industry or labor unions. To promote the myth of fairness this flaw is displayed as an asset. The choice of arbitrators are mutually agreed upon by the contract negotiators of the company and the international union, and they must carry impeccable credentials of neutrality if they desire to be chosen. They are well organized in the tightly-controlled American Arbitration Association and the National Academy of Arbitrators. Neither the workers or local unions are consulted or have any hand in selecting the arbitrator.

But, even if the arbitrators possessed all the omniscience they and their sponsors claim, they would be incapable of giving any meaning to the purposefully evasive grievance procedure, or of making it a source of justice in the workplace. Consider, for instance, that of the more than five hundred grievances filed in a single year by members of Local 1033 at the Republic Steel plant in South Chicago, fewer than twenty were heard in arbitration. About every three months, four or five grievances are submitted to arbitration.

In many workplaces, an arbitrator has *never* been called upon to settle a worker's grievance. The local union simply can't afford the luxury. Though the international union makes the decision as to whether a grievance may be submitted to arbitration, the local union is required to pay the costs (shared equally with the company). One arbitration hearing can run into costs of thousands of dollars. Union treasuries of smaller locals having only a few hundred members (and these are in the majority) aren't able to meet these costs.

Nationally, it is estimated that of the 200,000 to 300,000 grievances from the workplace filed each year, only two percent of these reach arbitration.

In every workplace throughout the land, wherever collective bargaining has established a grievance procedure, the industrial relations offices and the grievancemen's pockets are bulging with pink, and blue, and white, grievance papers that are shuffled around from step to step, and then back again, until, except for a trifling number that are speculated to be acts of company charity or fragments of a covert formula to persuade skeptics, they are ultimately withdrawn by the local union or contractually denied by the company. The acid truths of collective bargaining are spoken by the unresolved grievances of the blue collar workers in the workplaces of America.

The Workplace and Its Discontents

The reports that follow are factual accounts of grievances and complaints from the workplace. They are part of the written and verbal record of an estimated one thousand similar grievances and complaints filed every work-day throughout the United States, wherever there are provisions for filing, in the mills, mines, factories, terminals, construction sites, stores, docks, railroad yards, refineries, hospitals, orchards and other sites where workers toil.

They are presented to reveal the inner landscape of the workplace, and because they are the materials that are most needed by anyone wishing to make sense out of blue collar studies. The enduring qualities of the blue collar workers, their fitness as individuals, their attachments to customs and institutions, their views of themselves and their work, their families, their union, their class, are shaped, primarily, in the workplace. (We are what we do.)

Some might be tempted to compare these accounts with the "case studies" of social researchers and therapists. However, they are fundamentally and critically different, in that here there are no "patients", or no clinical staff, and relatively few concerns with guilt. There was no professional analyst or licensed healer who sat and took notes while the subjects reeled out their discontents. These accounts are from an active worker who worked side by side with the others, griped and grieved with them over the same "lousy" conditions, walked the picket lines with them when there was a strike, ate, drank and spent days off with them and their families, was attended by the same company doctor when injured on the job, was "pushed" by the same bosses, and, off and on, when elected, served as their union grievanceman. And the relief sought through these complaints was economic justice rather than mental therapy.

Many of the grievances discussed here occurred repeatedly at different times and with different workers, and under slightly varying circumstances. In such events, the particular incident selected was the one that was made up of the most intimately known circumstances and of the most studied investigation.

There is no pretense here to have researched the three hundred thousand grievances filed yearly throughout the nation's workplaces. But even a surface examination of workers' grievances from many different plants and industries demonstrates how comfortably they all fit into a familiar pattern. Though conditions, and occupations, and work rules, and contract language, and ethnic formation, may vary in the workplaces, there emerges a singular uniformity in work and in the interactions between workers and management.

Chapter Nine

Rigged!

A highly respected labor arbitrator for more than twenty years, Paul R. Hayes, after his appointment to the federal bench, confided, in a lecture at the Yale University Law School (*Storrs Lectures on Jurisprudence*) that "We know a large portion of the awards of arbitrators are rendered by incompetents, that another proportion—we don't know how large but are permitted by the circumstances to suspect that it is quite large—is rendered on the basis of what award might be best for the arbitrator's future. We know there is another group of cases...in which the arbitrator has rendered a rigged award."

Shocking, perhaps, to the delicate senses of the Yale students. But, to blue collar workers who find themselves in a scrape with the boss, or believe they have been deprived of their seniority rights, or have been unjustly disciplined, or discriminated against on account of their race or national origin or sex, and pin their hopes on the grievance procedure and the labor arbitrator, it's a confession that seriously reduces the collective bargaining system in the workplace.

If it is forbidden, as it is, in practically all labor contracts, for the workers to strike during the term of the contract (and, in some contracts even beyond its date of expiration) and the workers are denied the opportunity to approve or disapprove the contract negotiated for them by their international union officers, and the grievance machinery is groaning to a halt for want of good-faith collective bargaining on the plant level, and, finally, the ultimate blow, to discover that the keystone of the entire structure, the labor arbitrator, is incompetent, corrupt, and self-serving, it would seem enough grounds for the blue collar workers to seek other, more decent, means to settle the problems in the workplace.

Wilbert D. Fleming, clock number 31840, a one-time wire-drawer in the wire mill of Republic Steel, can attest that power mis-used by a labor arbitrator is no less wicked and harmful to a worker than power mis-used by the corporation. Of course, it is out of the question that Clock Number 31840 could come to Yale and lecture the law students about his experience with labor arbitration, but it could be important to their education.

The arbitration decision in the discharge of Wilbert D. Fleming, handed down from the Office of the Umpire, (indexed Number SW-38) confirms everything Judge Paul Hayes told the Yale students about "incompetent" arbitrators who hand down decisions "that might be best for the arbitrator's future," and render "rigged awards."

The language and the facts in the Fleming award are taken directly from the arbitrator's written decision. By itself, and without the record of the proceedings, it gives a fair and sufficient account of the thinking and manners of the arbitrator.

The hearing was held six months after Fleming had been fired from his job as a wire-drawer for allegedly assaulting his foreman in the wire mill. Before it reached the arbitrator a grievance protesting the discharge was heard by the industrial relations department of the plant, but to nobody's surprise it upheld the company. The union grievanceman argued that the foreman wasn't telling the truth (it's never proper, in grievance meetings with the company, to call anyone a liar), that the company's story was contradictory, that Fleming had a good work record, that there were serious overtones of racial prejudice in the discharge. It seemed these arguments served only to harden the company's position. It insisted that Republic "has had it with Fleming," That their decision was "final and irrevocable," that it was "a savage and unprovoked assault on a supervisor", that the union was engaging in "rabble-rousing" and that the company was steadfastly devoted to racial equality. If a white employee assaulted a Negro foreman, we would do it the same way, said the company superintendent.

Though the civil rights act had already been signed by the President, there had been a virtual epidemic of discharges of Black employees in the plant, and it took some pressures before the international union agreed to appeal this one to arbitration. It was time, way past time, for a stand against the high rate of discharges of Black workers.

The arbitrator's decision declared, "At issue here is the propriety of the discharge of Wilbert D. Fleming, a wire mill department employee with 3½ years seniority for allegedly assualting Robert S. Pearson, foreman of the wire-drawers.

"Although there were sharp conflicts in the testimony of the witnesses, and patent departures from the truth in at least two instances, the essential facts of the case are set forth below.

"The grievant, Fleming, a wire drawer, was found by his foreman Robert S. Pearson, away from his work area and Pearson remonstrated with him over that fact. Fleming replied with an excuse which did not satisfy Pearson (he had gone to the toilet), and words were exchanged in a rising crescendo during which Fleming levelled the term 'M——F——' at Pearson and offered to 'meet him outside.'

"Pearson, on his part, called Fleming a 'low class Nigger' and 'black scum of the earth.' Pearson's claim that he limited his epithets to 'low-down colored' was sharply contradicted by Fleming and lacks the ring of veracity.

"It is undisputed that twice during the exchange Fleming (the grievant) sought to break off the encounter by turning around and walking off. However, on each occasion Pearson followed Fleming.

"There is a sharp dispute over whether Pearson then grabbed Fleming's shirt near his collar, as Fleming claims, or whether Pearson put his hand on Fleming's chest to hold off Fleming from crowding him, as Pearson asserts.

"In any case, what happened next is perfectly clear. Fleming pushed Pearson, knocking him on his back and then bent over him and struck him in the face. Pearson suffered a broken nose, a chipped tooth, and cuts on his face requiring stitches. Fleming's assertion that he did not strike Pearson and the latter fell when Fleming pushed Pearson's hands off after Pearson grabbed his shirt was patently false."

(Here, let us digress from the arbitrator's reasoning, to insert an important piece of information that the arbitrator didn't consider weighty enough to mention. There were two workers from the wire mill who testified at the arbitration hearing, and gave the same version of the incident as Fleming's, while the company didn't produce any witnesses for their version. Ordinarily, witnesses, and especially company witnesses, have a decisive influence on arbitration hearings. But the arbitrator's characterization of Fleming's own account as "patently false" applied with equal force to the testimony of Fleming's inexpert witnesses. In examining past arbitration rulings that were decided on the basis of the veracity of witnesses, a marked tilt towards the company witnesses is manifest. It is indeed rare that a blue collar worker's word is believed above that of a supervisor's.)

"For striking the foreman, Fleming was discharged. His prior record was average or better and was free of disciplinary infractions," the arbitrator continued.

"The question is whether Fleming's discharge should be sustained. In an ordinary case of an assault on a supervisor, there is little question that the discharge penalty is in order.

Management must be assured that its supervisors will be able to function without fear for their personal safety. An employee whose self-control, even under considerable provocation, is so limited that he is prompted to resort to fisticuffs is hardly equipped to withstand the stresses of factory life and in the usual case his removal from employment is justified if he assaults a foreman.

"In this case, however, we have two special components which should be taken into account. The first is that Foreman Pearson failed to forestall the incident by breaking off contact when Fleming hurled a verbal insult at him. Instead of ordering Fleming to report to his office for discipline and leaving the scene, Pearson pressed the matter not only by replying with epithets of his own but by pursuing Fleming when the latter twice tried to break away. Moreover he made the mistake of initiating body contact by either grasping Fleming's shirt or placing his hands on Fleming's chest, an act which is in any case likely to be inflamatory.

"But even this would not in the ordinary case mitigate the gravity of the offense of assault on a supervisor. We are given pause, however, by the second component of this case, namely the use by Pearson of racial epithets in response to Fleming's verbal insults directed at him.

"If supervisors in industrial plants should have learned anything from the turmoil over civil rights and over the justified demands of Negroes for equal treatment of the past decade, they should have learned that it is absolutely essential to refrain from racial slurs in talking to employees of another color or ethnic background. A supervisor who has not mastered that simple truth and who cannot forebear giving voice to his innate prejudices can scarcely lay claim to the fullest measure of immunities that should attach to his status. A racial insult, in the fragile and tenuous state of race relations currently can be as dangerous as a match in a hayloft and is a provocation that no one should engage in.

"When the matter at hand is thus viewed, one cannot justify Fleming's act of striking Pearson, but one can understand the nature of the pressures generated by the entire incident. In no cases are assaults on supervision justified, and when they occur a severe measure of discipline is in order. But where, as here, the foreman had such a definite part in creating the atmosphere in which it occurred, I must in all fairness take that into account in determining the degree of discipline that is in order.

"Given all the circumstances I shall hold that a penalty lay-off from June 20 through January 7 is appropriate in Fleming's case. His reinstatement on January 8 shall be without back pay but without loss of seniority and it is suggested that the parties make all efforts to place him on a job under someone else's supervision if possible."

The decision was signed by Saul Wallen and Bert Luskin, two highly entrenched and influential arbitrators, selected repeatedly for more than twenty years by both the international officers of the steelworkers union and the industrial relations department of the steel corporation. But, as federal judge Hayes, nursing twenty years of labor arbitration under his black robe, confided to the Yale students of law arbitrator's decisions, a large portion of them, at least, are willfull and shifty, and are rendered on the basis of "what might be best for the arbitrator's future." And, since the fate and fortunes of labor arbitrators flow smoothly in the same stream with corporate management, and there is absolutely no chance of their survival without benefit of the life-line fastened to the company's industrial relations department, what is best for them can be ruinous to a blue collar worker.

The wire-drawer gave up six month's pay. The company, as we shall see, gave up nothing, and got exactly what it wanted. The union, desperately needing to prove its opposition to the extreme disciplining of Black steelworkers, reported to its membership that the Fleming decision was a victory; the discharge was overturned. And the arbitrator, predictably, was selected by the international union and the corporation for another three year term of the labor agreement.

The arbitration decision is quoted at length because a large part of the ignorance about labor arbitration on this continent is because labor arbitrators are so seldom seen in public, and their activities are so veiled in mystery. Except, possibly, for a government-appointed arbitration panel on an issue of national economic and political consequence, they are largely unnoticed by the media. The decision in the discharge grievance of Wilbur Fleming, clock number 31840, or of any other blue collar worker, is as unlikely a subject of a newspaper column as yesterday's weather forecast. Even the workers involved don't get a copy of the decision to read.

It doesn't require expertise in the arbitration profession, nothing more than common sense, to see that nowhere in western civilization, not even in the armed forces, does there prevail a system of such flawless discipline as the arbitrator has assumed for the workplace. What crime did Fleming commit by "being away from his work area?" Was it like "fleeing under fire" during wartime? Fleming's job was not an assembly-line operation where a replacement may be required when a worker must leave for one reason or another. Wire-drawers frequently leave their machines for short spells to get a cup of coffee, go to the toilet, to get a whiff of cool air at an open door, to answer a phone call, without accounting to anyone for their absence. Unless it is overdone. Clearly, it was the intimidating and insulting line of questions from a racially prejudiced foreman, reflecting a racially prejudiced department, in a racially prejudiced workplace, in a racially prejudiced corporation, that triggered the entire affair.

Did a labor arbitrator ever pose the question whether a racially prejudiced supervisor for a racially prejudiced corporation should be required to promote civil rights? It would be interesting to get an opinion.

On which ghetto street did the arbitrator learn that Fleming's use of the term "motherfucker" was an "insult" and the foreman's use of the term "nigger" was an "epithet?"

What immunities are bestowed on a foreman, and by whom? If the arbitrator was convinced, as he said, that the foreman pursued Fleming and made the first bodily contact with him, most any reasonable human being other than adherents of "no fault" morality, would say it was the fault of the foreman if a fight developed. But when the arbitrator came to making the final decision he said it was the worker's fault, and punished him with six month's loss of pay. If it were the other way around, if Fleming had pursued the foreman and made the first bodily contact, there's no question what the arbitrator would rule. It would be the end of Fleming.

It has never seriously been suggested, but what legal principle or natural law places a management person or a corporation executive beyond the reach of the labor arbitrator, like say, a couple of month's off without pay? Sounds silly! But why? Aren't both parties in the collective bargaining process supposed be equal?

The final, and quintessential element, the kernel of the rigging in the arbitrator's decision, is that the wire-drawer job at this plant had been, for as long as there was a wire mill there, a *white job,* and Fleming was the first and only Black to be assigned to it. This was a vital industrial and social statistic which the arbitrator well knew, and should have noted. All that jazz about how supervisors in industry "should have learned that it is absolutely essential to refrain from racial slurs in talking to employees of another color" is a pretty thin cover for a half-century of racial discrimination in the wire mill.

The union staffman told the local union it was a victory for Fleming. But, while the union did save his job, the life result of the arbitrator's award was a good deal less than a victory.

Fleming had never pictured himself in a toe to toe battle with the company over racial matters, or over any other matters. All he wanted was to work at his trade, be paid what he was worth, drink with his friends, raise his family, love his wife, and be left alone. Strange, how an insignificant walk to the washroom to empty one's bladder can flatten a blue collar worker.

He waited twenty-eight weeks for the arbitrator's ruling on his discharge, confident, somehow, as are most workers, that the ruling would make things right again. For twenty-eight weeks he didn't get a paycheck, and went deeply into debt. He, naively, counted on the retroactive pay that he was certain the arbitrator would order "as soon as he squeezed the truth out of that m-----f-----foreman." He had heard, and, in fact, it was written into the union contract, though he hadn't personally read it, that when a worker is unjustly fired, the company pays the worker all the earnings he lost. He didn't want to believe there were tricky little words in the contract that had the diabolical power to wipe out the simplest rights and most legitimate claims of the blue collar worker, and that the retroactive pay he was banking on would become real only if the arbitrator saw fit and ordered it paid. In this decision, as in most, there was no such order. Not a single penny of back pay. The six month loss of earnings was a punishment, like a fine or an extra charge, for, for . . . well, for having dirty thoughts about the foreman!

Fleming, in accord with the arbitrator's ruling, was transferred out of the wire-drawer's department, thus restoring it to its previous "white" status, just as the company wanted it, without any further trouble from "low-class coloreds." The foreman would no longer need to harken to the arbitrator's advice to "refrain from making racial slurs," because with Fleming gone, who would take offense?

Here and there in labor arbitration, one does come across arbitrators who stand out from the others for their extraordinary insight into the workplace. The arbitrators in the Fleming discharge have, on other occasions, occupied such a spot. Grievously for Fleming, this probably was, though there is no proof, a command performance, in which the arbitrators rendered an award, in Judge Hayes' terms "on the basis of what might be best for the arbitrator's future." This is not a polemic. It's a documentary. But it has to be said: "a rigged decision, if there ever was one!"

Chapter Ten

Nine Cents Ain't the World.

1969, predicted once to become the "year of the moon," found corporate industry much more narrowly concerned with an earthly problem, much closer to home. It was *workers' productivity*—the well-spring of profits (according to an economic theory universally condemned by corporate boards). An alarm was being broadcasted that America was losing the race in that most important sector of the Free World. Divide the number of tons of steel produced in American mills by the number of steelworkers employed, and then do the same for Japanese steel mills. What do you get? As suspected, the Japanese were clobbering the Americans no less fiercely than at Pearl Harbor, and if anyone at this late date doubted the military theory of the renowned Clausewitz, that war is an extension of politics, this was compelling evidence.

Industry and Labor leaders, sharing a common goal, as they said, made the competitiveness of American industry their common concern. It must have taken great intellectual effort for some at the steelworkers union convention that year, to accept, with such consummate grace and enthusiasm, the "fraternal greetings" offered by the visiting delegates of the Japanese steelworkers union, and to respond so earnestly in endorsing the lofty ideals of international labor solidarity, while at that very moment an agreement was being reached in Washington to keep Japaneses steel out of the country. Only in the minds of impractical and doctrinaire unionists was this a laborious hurdle. No sweat, if the rubbish of the *international brotherhood of labor* is carted away.

That unions in America are *international* and are sworn to the defense of workers of all nations is a terrible misunderstanding. They are called *international unions* only because they have members in Canadian industry (generally owned by American corporations). Otherwise the international unions of the AFL-CIO have no members outside the United States, or its possessions. Distinct from other trade unions over the world, the AFL-CIO is not even affiliated to any international federation or world body of labor, not even the International Labor Organization (ILO) which works in partnership with the United Nations. On this it is to the right of the State Department.

From the precious principle of *Workers of the World, Unite!* to the furiously decadent *Buy American* (filched from the KKK) was a long and tortuous trail for Labor. But the AFL-CIO made it, and strangely, in the lead was the officialdom of those international unions (ILGWU, Textile, Amalgamated Clothing Workers) who had always been first to spring up with gusto, some even with fists clenched, to sing *Solidarity Forever.*

Now, to return to the workplace (it always seems so far away from where labor policy is made), it was in that year of 1969 that Republic Steel Corporation in South Chicago, in pursuit of greater productivity, installed a new scarfing machine in its blooming mill. It's not absolutely essential for our story to be familiar with the details of its workings, any more than it's required to understand the mathematical equations of Galileo to appreciate his confrontation with the Church, but a brief sketch of this new scarfing machine should be helpful.

It's a fascinating, electronically-controlled system. It does the work of seventy steelworkers scarfing by hand, and requires only one lower-paid employee to operate the controls, and a small maintenance crew to keep it from burning up or breaking down.

Jetting blasts of white flame from the nozzles of four banks of sixty-four acetylene torches line up, hugging closely to the sides of the ingot as it travels along the mill rolls, and *scarfs,* or peels off, from the ingot its useless outer-layer of metalurgical skin.

From the very beginning, the scarfer repairmen, special and different from millwrights or other maintenance personnel, were removed from any line of progression, or seniority sequence in the plant. It was a special occupation to which or from which there is no opening. The company was not bound in any manner in hiring scarfer repairmen. Nobody had the right to "bid" on the job. They all came from the gatehouse, at the discretion of the company. That's unusual in a plant with a union organization. But, until federal law illegalized such a closed system of seniority, no undesireables touched that machine. It was protected from mongrelization as tightly as the moon-landing.

Workers in the plant understood that the scarfer repairman job was reserved for the pets of the company. It was cleaner than the millwright or motor inspector's job. They weren't required to respond to mill-whistles. They had their own repair shop, where the bosses would stop and be served coffee. The job didn't pay quite as much as other maintenance people, but there were so many other advantages the company could strictly screen people for the job.

With the installation of the new machine the scarfer repairmen's status zoomed. They were suddenly receiving extraordinary attention from the big wheels in the company, treated almost like partners in a new industrial conquest. They were given special instruction and training by the manufacturer on the care and upkeep of their machine. A new set of skills were required for the job, including brazing, hydraulics, electronics—all kinds of stuff that wasn't required from ordinary repairmen and millwrights. The transition from the old to the new machine became quite an enterprise, with dozens of white-hatted superintendents, engineers, time-study men, and specialists of all kinds crowding around the scarfing machine, making notes, asking questions, clucking, nodding.

The scarfer repairmen were being smothered with flattery for their star roles in this new advance in steel technology. Almost daily they got assurances that they would be fittingly rewarded for their new responsibilities. "This job should be raised to Class 18, at least," was whispered confidentially almost daily into their ears. (That would have established a 63¢ an hour raise, from $3.512 to $4.142.)

For a time, the scarfer repairmen's lives in the plant were being gossiped about in latrines and locker-rooms. Where did these guys come from, and what are they doing, besides brown-nosing? They had their own shop, with a sign on the door DO NOT ENTER. You'd think it was Cape Kennedy! They worked as much overtime as they pleased. They were practically their own bosses. They made their own work schedules. They did their own ordering of parts and materials, elsewhere the exclusive function of management. They had a burner in their shop to cook their lunches. They put on a newly-laundered set of work-clothes every day, on the excuse that grease on their clothes could cause an accident. Inside the shop was stacked several binders of company pamphlets on the care and maintenance of the scarfing machine, and, often, they locked themselves in, studying the pamphlets, so they said. Accusations that they were reading pornographic magazines on overtime were never dignified with a reply. If anyone would have preached to them about "humanizing the workplace," or the "blue collar blues," they probably would have thought them weird.

As so often happens in the workplace, when the newness of an up-to-date system or installation wears off, and the excite-

ment quiets down after its mysteries have been mastered, the
bosses are eager to be finally done with the fire-brigade type
of supervision and to settle back and reclaim their former routine. The scarfer repairmen couldn't help notice that, like yesterday's motion picture starlet, their glamour was beginning
to fade. Supervision, including their own immediate foreman,
seemed no longer attentive. Only when there was a major
breakdown on the scarfer machine did excitement rise again,
but more and more frequently the repairmen were being
blamed for the breakdowns. One of the millwrights shrewdly
observed that "the honeymoon was coming to an end." Supervision even stopped coming by their shop for coffee.

Many weeks passed, and it seemed everyone had forgotten
about the scarfer repairman's raise in pay. Months went by
and they were still working at their old rate of pay—job class
eleven, $3.512 per hour. They made diplomatic inquiries from
their foreman, who himself had once been a union grievanceman and could see their problem from both sides, and he told
them that, as far as he knew, the matter was being "studied"
by the industrial engineers. There's nothing much you can do,
except wait, they were repeatedly told.

Waiting isn't the same for all people. It depends on where
you stand, and how much shifting is allowed. It depends on
how desperately you need what or whom you are waiting for,
and how much you sweat. Patience is an intimate art for the
comfortable, for the fulfilled, for the strong, not for the blue
collar worker earning $3.512 an hour and each hour is losing
sixty three cents, and, like in a nightmare, the dollar bills are
floating away and you're in a state of paralysis.

They knew the risks in being too pushy, and rubbing the
front office the wrong way. They didn't want to spoil what
they had—the special indulgences, the overtime, no bosses
breathing down their backs. But without the raise in pay it
wasn't that great. They had more money coming to them and
nobody wants to be cheated. They had listened to the foreman, who they were certain was their friend, but his advice

didn't work out, and they doubted that he carried much weight in the company. Against his advice, they talked to their union grievanceman. After all, they paid union dues like the others, and they were entitled to help from their union.

The grievanceman told them, "Don't wait another day. File a grievance before you're too late." They thought of him as a "radical" but they suspected he was telling them the truth. He explained that the union contract says that when a new machine is installed which requires higher skills, the company is required to reclassify the job and pay the worker a higher rate of pay. The company had already agreed, but if the company stalls and there's no grievance on file, it becomes too late, and the grievance is thrown out for being *untimely* and that's the end of your raise in pay. It has happened just like that many, many, times in this plant.

(All grievances requesting reclassification of a job in the plant are referred to a committee called the *Plant Union Committee on Job Classification*—Article Five, Section Eleven of the Union Contract. This committee is made up of three industrial engineers of the company and three workers from the plant. The principal assets of the industrial engineers are said to be their total inability to communicate with the blue collar workers on the committee, and an unnatural passion for computing the simplest addition or subtraction with a slide rule. The opportunities for the blue collar workers on the committee to become job classification experts are further limited by the high rate of turn-over. They usually resign from the committee after a few months of service, frazzled by the pettiness, arrogance and the undisguised dallying of the company representatives. They are replaced, when available, with fresh, untrained, volunteers from the ranks of the local union, while the company representatives seem to last forever. And, with the slate clean, negotiations begin from a fresh start.)

Not completely convinced that their friends in supervision hadn't abandoned them, nor that the union could really help them, they signed (were talked into signing, they confessed to their foreman) a grievance requesting reclassification of their job, and "to be made whole for all lost earnings."

Such grievances in the workplace tend to be the most stubborn of all grievances. Other union grievances can, and generally do, fade away with the passing of time, a change in working conditions, a loss of sustained interest. Or the year-end thaw, where the union and the company, surveying the five hundred or so unsettled grievances, work out a face-saving "crash-program" of cancelling out grievances. But this hardly ever happens to a job-classification grievance. Workers on a job that is up for reclassification are reminded every payday that they have been ripped off. They greet their union grievanceman daily with "what's happening to our raise?" to which they get the same answer, "it's out of my hands. It's now in the hands of the Plant-Union committee."

That's how it went for two years for the scarfer repairmen, occasionally receiving an encouraging word from their foreman that he heard etcetera and etcetera, but nothing definite.

One day, after work, the repairmen went as a group to the office of the international union and talked with their man about their grievance. They got the same stumbling answers. It's in the hands of the committee. They're having meetings on it. There's nothing we can do here to speed it up. You have a good case, and it will be settled as soon as the company gets off its ass. The trouble is your local union people are filing so goddamn many grievances it's gumming up the whole works.

Next they went to see the superintendent of industrial relations. He shook his head, "Haven't they settled that damn thing yet?" He said he wasn't allowed to discuss it with them because it was already in the grievance procedure, but he promised he would do everything he could to speed up the settlement. He hinted, darkly, that the union was dragging its feet.

They sifted all that the union had told them and all the

company had told them, and they gathered nothing that they could cling to. It was what in the workplace, and other places, too, is called a run-around.

And then their friendly foreman told them he was going to stick his neck out, "cut through all the bullshit," and put through a raise for them. He would turn in their time to the payroll department as third-class millwrights, which would pay them nine cents an hour more. Labor grade twelve, instead of eleven. "Nine cents ain't the world," but that's as much as he, as a foreman can do. It's a simple time-sheet transaction, and it doesn't have to go through the front office. Don't talk to anybody about this, the foreman warned. And they understood that he meant not to talk to that "radical" grievanceman.

After a year, living high off the hog from the freakish 9¢ an hour raise, without benefit of union, of the contract, or the company, they heard from the inscrutable Plant-Union Committee on Job Classification. They heard it first from the company, that the international union and the company had reached a settlement, and that the scarfer repairman job had been raised to a class fifteen job. It was confirmed later by the union.

If there was no more to our report, and one didn't wish to make a mountain out of a three year cooling-off period, it could be considered a sort of vindication of the grievance procedure in the workplace, and even a fair case for slowing down fault-finding and griping against the international union staff.

But, behind the settlement of every job-classification grievance, there stands the frisky shadow of a retroactive lump-sum restitution. It's even more alluring than the prospect of the increased pay rate. The union contract provides that the workers shall be paid the sum of the difference between the earnings at the old rate and what it would have been under the new rate. The exact wording is "the resulting classification shall be effective as of the date when the new job was established or the change or changes installed." In the case of the scarfer machine, the "change or changes" were installed in 1969, and the settlement of the grievance was in 1972, an actual total of one hundred and seventy three weeks of retroactivity.

The scarfer repairmen had been told nothing about the size of their retroactive pay, but they knew expertly how to figure it. They calculated the regular hours, overtime hours, the six day weeks, the incentive differential, all the factors the payroll department would calculate, and they came up with a figure of *four thousand dollars*. It might have been more, but wherever there was doubt, they gave it to the company. Four thousand dollars was the *minimum* back pay due them. Not one of them had ever saved that much cash money, and the thought of it was sweet and overwhelming. It had the power to solve so many problems in their lives refinish the basement, a down-payment on a house, a new automobile, a long vacation trip—the things that we hear so many times from winners of sweepstake tickets.

They sweated it out four more weeks, and on a regular pay day they had a special note attached to their checks to see the paymaster for their "payment on Grievance No. S.C.26-69." At last!

Of course, as anyone could guess, when the paymaster handed them their check, it wasn't four thousand dollars. Not three, or two, or even one. Somehow, like an alchemist's mutation, their four thousand dollar gold nugget had shrunk to six hundred dollars gross (four hundred and eighty dollars after tax deductions).

If this comes on as a piddling matter, hardly a momentous social or moral issue, it is probably because work and wages, except for its broader implications of international negotiations or industry strikes, can become a pretty boring subject, like a soldier's experiences in basic training retold a hundred times. It's quite understandable that a shortage on the paychecks of a few workers isn't front page news. Not like the panic that sets in when one of great wealth loses his fortune.

But from the viewpoint of at least one of the aggrieved scarfer repairmen, who, almost daily, while munching on a sandwich, emphatically announces, "there's two things nobody better fuck with my lunch or my paycheck," a shortage of thirty four hundred dollars is definitely not boring.

In the workplace, employees on hourly wages seldom receive the same pay regularly. It will fluctuate from pay period to pay period, due to such factors as shift differentials, changes in incentive earnings, Sunday premium pay, overtime hours, payroll deductions, and these are frequently the basis of pay shortages. Within an hour after paychecks are distributed, lines of irate workers are clamoring at the door of the paymaster, demanding that they be paid the shortage "right now." They are convinced these shortages are intentional, and that every pay day the booty is pocketed by the company officials.

A shortage of thirty four hundred dollars is out of the ordinary, and clearly required more than a heated argument with the paymaster to straighten it out. This was no clerical error, no oversight on the scale of an unworked holiday or overtime premium. This was a half year's pay, a life time's saving, torn out of their hands by some devilish twist. It was a double-cross, a betrayal, a broken promise from the company they trusted and served so loyally.

They caught up with the local union president at the gate-house and demanded to know what happened to their retro-active pay. From then on it's like the script of a morality play. Every line is predictable. You know, I had nothing to do with your grievance. Go see Casey, the chairman of the Job-Classification committee.

Casey showed them the signed copy of the settlement. It was all there in black and white, with the superintendent of industrial relations' and the international staffman's signature. Here, I have a xerox copy. You take it.

The agreement read that the scarfer repairmen would be

reclassified and upgraded four labor grades, from class eleven to class fifteen. The men didn't quarrel with that. But, it read further that the scarfer repairmen would be paid retroactively for a period of *eighteen months* not forty months as it should have read.

But what about the union contract, that provides retroactive pay from the first day the job was changed? Those changes were forty months ago, not eighteen.

And six hundred dollars for eighteen month's back-pay? That's a crock. That's no more than six month's back-pay. Figure it out for yourself.

After being told that it wasn't the local union people that cheated them, that the international union handled the settlement, they were let in on the mysteries of collective bargaining. They were told the company *absolutely* refused to pay any more than eighteen months of back pay. If the union didn't go along, it might take another three years until it would reach arbitration. And who knows which way it would be decided? Yeah, you might call it a compromise. That's what we always have to do. They give a little, we give a little. You can't expect the company to give up everything. Half a loaf is better than none! If it were my money, I'd probably feel different. But, I swear, that was the best we could get.

But the mystery within the mystery —the whittling down of the agreed eighteen months to about six months retroactive pay. How did they figure that? Can't something be done about that?

The company had the figures. During twelve months of that eighteen months, the repairmen were being carried on the payroll as *millwrights* and *not* desurfacer repairmen. That was by private arrangement with their foreman, so he could get them a nine cent an hour raise in pay. A millwright isn't a desurfacer repairman. Millwrights aren't included in the agreement for retroactive pay. That's too bad, but it's the way the cookie crumbled.

A worker shouldn't need to be a Philadelphia lawyer to collect the proper pay. The union contract shouldn't be so tricky that it can wipe out a worker's earnings.

They discovered they had one more throw of the dice. They would go "downtown" to the United States Labor Board, and file a complaint against both the company and the union. They thought they would get justice here.

After several months of waiting, they received a letter from the government board that there was no violation of the labor laws, "no unfair labor practice," as charged. The letter said the government considered the case "closed." That wasn't easy for them to take. They thought they had a friend in the Labor Board. The local union boasted that it has never lost a case where a member had lodged a complaint against it, which could be interpreted as a pitiful misfortune for the workers, or a legend of the union's fidelity.

Chapter Eleven

Can't Sell Out My Mind

Chico had worked for Republic Steel about three years, starting as a welder's helper—the first, and, at that time, the only Chicano in that department. He climbed rapidly up the promotional ladder, to become a welder third class, second class, and then to the top, first class. He was uncomfortably aware that the company's rush to promote him was not because he was such a hot-shot welder, but was, more likely, his "minority status." The federal government was breathing down the company's back. But, that aside, considering his short experience, Chico was a pretty good welder, and most department foremen were well-satisfied when he would be assigned to their department on repair-turns or emergency breakdowns. Welders in steel mills are primarily maintenance workers, not on production, who are assigned daily to different departments in the plant for whatever repair work is needed. Their contact with their own department supervision is reduced to the barest essentials, administrative, not occupational, and they are like aliens wherever they are assigned, frequently the victims of crabby supervisors looking for a scapegoat to blame for their own blunders. Chico didn't feel more of an outsider or more set-upon than many of the other welders. Here and there, on occasions, he did encounter, from the lips of other despised ethnics, the familiar Anglo scorn for Latinos, but he had been hardened to this, and never having counted on genetic purity for support in life, accepted the slights as a perverse source of strength.

On the unhappy day Chico was escorted out of the plant by the plant guards, discharged, defrocked, exiled, he had been working with a crew of welders in the thirty-two inch mill, welding pedestals inside the re-heat furnace. There was nothing unusual about that job. He had done it many times before. It couldn't be rushed. Safety and health had to be carefully taken into account. The temperature in the furnace, even after it had been cooling for a whole day and night, was still so blasted hot that welders could do no more than jump in for three or four minutes at a time to pour a few rods, and then jump out for relief, to allow the sweat to cool their limbs and give the boiling blood a chance to course through their veins.

But the temperature inside the furnace or conditions of work weren't the cause of Chico's devastating misfortune that day, except in an oblique and adventitious way. That day the welders and other craftsmen working on the furnace, instead of eating their lunch inside the plant, as they are supposed to, sneaked off to the tavern across the highway. There's nothing like a cold beer at lunch to renew a body that's been in a hot furnace too long. However, Chico remained behind. Not solely because it was against the rules to leave the plant for lunch (though he was always careful about company rules, and on this particular noon he had a vague notion he was being watched) but he had decided to attend to a very serious matter during lunch time.

Here it is essential to know that Chico had recently been named by the local union as the employee representative on the *Contracting-Out Committee.* Actually, he had volunteered. The union's previous representative on the committee had resigned (in disgust!) and the union had a hard job convincing someone to serve. But Chico, somewhere in his young life (he was twenty-one and this was his only experience in an industrial plant) had become drawn to the labor movement. His father had been transported in a box-car from Mexico to work in the U. S. Steel plant during the 1919 steel strike, and that was the only hereditary factor in his attachment to unions. But he spoke with personal pride, familiarly, as if of a brother or father, of Chicano martyrs, of Juarez, Villa, and Cesar Chavez, the farmworkers' hero. He was delighted, eager, to become a member of a union committee that watched over the rights of his fellow-workers.

Under the provisions of the union contract (Section Six, of Article Five) a joint committee of management and union was established to oversee the company's contracting out of work. The *Contracting-Out-Committee* was the outcome of many years of complaints that repair and fabricating work which properly should be done by the company's regular employees, was being contracted out to other companies, which resulted in lay-offs and short work weeks for the regular employees. The union contract specified that, "Before the Company finally decides to contract out a significant item of work . . . the union committee will be notified . . . (and) the management members of the committee shall give full consideration to any comments or suggestions by the union members of the committee . . . "

Whoever has had experience in union grievance activities, or in trying to make sense out of the language of union contracts, will immediately recognize this clause as meaningless clutter which so often substitutes for candor in collective bargaining. In no sense does it give the union any rights to control or prevent any contracting out that the company has decided upon. The company agrees only "to give full consideration to any comments or suggestions," which is only a hair's distance from doing as they damn well please. Workers on the committee soon discover they are pawns without any power, and resign. There's always an opening for a union member on the *contracting-out committee*, and that was Chico's invitation to test whether a blue collar worker and an ardent trade union activist can occupy the same space in the workplace.

Chico had observed during that morning that one of the trucks of an outside contractor was loading a pile of steel slabs. He recognized this material as the same he had worked on together with boilermakers in fabricating skids for the various furnaces in the plant. It was being shipped out for fabrication by another company—a matter that Chico considered within the scope of the contracting-out committee. That was the main reason he didn't accompany the other welders to the tavern during lunch that day. He was intensely serious about his position on the union committee. Workers were convinced (and this was a couple of years before aircraft and oil corporations admitted to paying and receiving bribes, and before top-level management people at the Burns Harbor, Indiana Bethlehem Steel plant were fired in a multimillion-dollar construction kick-back scandal) that "pay-olla" was being collected from the work being contracted out. Furthermore, as a welder, he, himself, was being deprived of a possible extra day's work whenever an outside contractor did their jobs.

(Aside from the collective bargaining issue, this dispute serves to illustrate basically competing approaches in labor-management relations. Management, generally, claims that individuals engaging in collective bargaining should be detached, not involved personally, and that a union committeeman, who, like Chico, is selfishly identified with a specific settlement of a grievance, should not be a part of the labor-management committee to settle the grievance. Absurd and hypocritical as such views may appear on close inspection, most international union officials do not care to disagree. In order to keep aggrieved workers at a safe distance away from the process of settling grievances in the workplace, the union contract provides only for the most cursory hearings in the "lower steps" of the grievance procedure, which might include face-to-face meeting with the workers. Afterwards, the grievance is transferred to the "higher steps." In the higher steps there is an entirely new element in the works. It is the union staffman, not workers who are employed by the company, who handles the grievance for the employees. The staffman is appointed, not elected. Staffmen consider themselves "technicians" or "labor specialists," not workers. They are accountable to the international union, not to members of a local union in the plant. They are based in the headquarters of the international union in Pittsburgh, Detroit, Washington, and other urban centers, not in workplaces of America.)

While the welders were on their lunch time, the superintendent began inspecting the work that had been done that morning in the furnace, and Chico, his heart in his throat, and with all the respectful manners a welder, weighed down with gear and safety equipment, could gather, addressed him, "Sir, as a member of the contracting-out committee, would you tell me why those skids in 'D Bay' are being sent outside?"

It could have been that the superintendent was disgruntled over the amount of work that had been done in the furnace, or it might have been a quick reaction against the outlawed "union business during working hours." Although he was on the same committee with Chico, supposedly as equals, there was never even the most elementary rapport existing between them. The superintendent flew into a rage, and shouted, "Get back on your job. You don't know what-in-hell you're talking about. I've been watching you, and you've been sitting on your dead cock all morning. To me you're no different than the rest of those wet-backs." What else he shouted at Chico isn't too certain.

Chico answered as calmly as he could, "I'm on my lunch time. Right now I am representing the union for the contracting-out committee."

What happened next is a matter of whom you believe—a blue collar worker or a department superintendent. The accounts are contradictory. The union contract doesn't establish a system of weights and measures, or psychic guidelines to fish out the truth and trap the lie. In most spheres of society these days, platforms of truth are pretty shaky, anyhow. So, in the workplace, where the inequality of worker and management is so pronounced, how does one balance the word of a blue collar worker against that of a superintendent? Union staffmen, with life-styles and ambitions often indistinguishable from management, privately confess it is easier for them to believe management's version than a worker's, and they whitewash their bias with the subtle commentary that "a worker in trouble would be stupid to tell the truth."

According to Chico—and this is exactly how he told it at hearing after hearing—the superintendent, continuing with obscenities, grabbed him by the shoulder and tried to push him. Chico brushed his hand off him. The superintendent lost his balance, slipped and fell on a pile of scrap strewn about the area in front of the furnace. His white hard-hat fell off. Chico recovered it, wiped it off, and handed it to him. He asked if he was hurt. The superintendent grabbed the hard-hat, wiped it again, and without a word, strode off. (Even if it does sound like a scenario, a model defense, regularly pleaded and rarely accepted at discharge hearings, that doesn't make it untrue, if it is in fact true. Poets and philosophers hold that Truth is bigger than Fact, but they are not likely witnesses at discharge hearings.)

Chico sat down in the shearman's pulpit, an enclosure, perched over the mill rolls, which usually housed the crew which sized and cut the hot ingots. Since it was a repair-turn, the crew was off and Chico was afforded an opportunity to be alone, to relax, cool off, think over what hapened, and eat a sandwich. He opened his lunch-bucket, but he wasn't hungry. He was restless and chilled. He felt his heart pounding. He knew enough about the mill to calculate that the explosive events of the day weren't over, and that they were bound to build up to some kind of climax.

The superintendent, more composed, wholly experienced in the handling of recalcitrant blue collar workers, wasted no time or motion, and went directly to the office of Industrial

Relations. There he gave one of the counselors a statement, taken down, and polished, it is suspected, with potent editorial corrections, and typed in triplicate. It, too, was a model deposition—the kind that originated the court-room phrase, "as phony as an eyewitness"—embarrasingly flawless, but with the advantage of a superintendent's reputation to bolster it. (That, to be fair, doesn't make it untrue either, if it is, in fact, true.)

The superintendent's version held that he was making a routine inspection of the furnace repairs in the thirty-two inch mill, and he told one of the welders, Chico, that work on the furnace was too slow, and he wanted a better showing in the afternoon. Chico answered that it was too hot in the furnace, and then changed the subject to inquire about some work he said was being contracted out. The superintendent, however, brought the conversation back to the matter of the furnace. Then Chico became abusive, and shouted, "I'm not going to let you get away with this!" The superintendent replied, "This isn't the place to argue. We're here to work," and he turned away to leave. Chico spun him around and punched him, knocking him down. Then he kicked him in the head with his steel-toed safety shoes, bruising and cutting him about the face. (That was the account the superintendent stuck to, rigidly, in every phase of the subsequent union-company hearings, without ever yielding as much as a comma.)

After he left the office of Industrial Relations, he notified the weld-shop foreman to write out an official discharge notice for Chico, effective immediately.

Then, a call to Plant Protection to pick up Chico at the shearman's pulpit in the thirty-two inch mill and escort him out of the plant. Precise, and strictly in accord with "past practice" in the plant. Procedurally, there was no deviation from the labor contract.

In the dark days of industrial barbarism, before the acceptance of labor unions, and before discharge procedures were established by agreement between management and labor, that would have closed the book for Chico, and this would be the end of our report. (Unless, of course, one chooses, in tune with the bicentennial celebrations, to contrast it to the old order in colonial New England, where discharge from employment was considered inadequate for a worker "who laid violent hands upon his master," and the employer had the option of additional penalties, including "burning his tongue with a hot iron," public floggings and jail terms.)

Chico, by union contract, was entitled to a "hearing." Discharges, until officially and finally upheld in the course of grievance procedure, are only "provisional." In workplaces with union contracts, "pre-emptory" discharges are forbidden. However, considering that a provisionally discharged worker, in the period of weeks and months waiting for a final decision either sustaining or rescinding the provisional discharge, is cut off, completely, from all the rights of an employee, and has no earnings, no vacation rights, no hospital or medical coverage, no unemployment benefits, this distinction is often more theoretical than real. Nonetheless, only a crank would deny that workers have improved their positions in respect to employment security through union organization, just as only a fool would believe that workers no longer need to worry about being unjustly fired from their jobs.

The first hearing on Chico's discharge was held in the office of the company's industrial relations department. Present was Chico, his union grievanceman, the superintendent who fired him, three assistants to the superintendent of industrial relations, and a stenographer out of the industrial relations office. Sophisticated union grievancemen view the first hearing as a mere formality, cut-and-dried, possibly a chance to find out the company's intentions. It is commonly understood that if the word hasn't already filtered down that the company is prepared to rescind the discharge "without prejudice to either party," the first hearing is only for the technical purpose of appealing the discharge to the third step of the grievance procedure, and then to the fourth step, where the restraining hand of the international union staffman takes over for the discharged worker and for the local union in the workplace. It is in the fourth step, without the personal, selfish, excitable presence of these directly involved in the grievance, that the hard decision is made whether to appeal the discharge to arbitration, rescind or sustain the discharge. (Labor studies showing that a fair share of discharges are invalidated by labor arbitrators—the usual figure claimed is twenty-five per cent—do not reflect the real situation: namely, that only a trifling number of the thousands of discharges each year ever reach the stage of arbitration. The great bulk of them are surrendered to the company in the earlier hearings and grievance procedures.)

In the Chico discharge there was no sign from the company that it would be ready to reach a settlement, and hardly to anyone's surprise, the discharge was sustained in all the stages of hearings and was appealed to the fourth step, where serious discussions might possibly take place.

The firing of Chico became a subject of more than usual comment in the plant. To the workers, the issue clearly became one of company reprisal against an active union man, not one of a worker assaulting a supervisor. Especially in the weld-shop, where discipline was a perpetual problem, and few employees had escaped its net, the employees sensed that the firing of Chico placed them all in jeopardy, and they called a meeting of the shopmen in defense of Chico (a rare move, not ordinary procedure in a unionized plant). Those who suppose a blue collar worker's speech is limited to the familiar expletives and cliches of the tavern might have been startled by the stinging fluency of the welders who spoke out in Chico's defense, denouncing the "dirty tricks of the company." In more subtle tones, the union came in for a share of the blame. "If the union can't defend Chico, what can it do for the rest of us?"

Chico stood up beside his chair and told his fellow-workers what had happened in front of the furnace. "If I had turned my head the other way while outside contractors were stealing our work, I wouldn't be in this mess." He told them the company had made up its entire story. Not a single word of truth in it. "No arbitrator would believe that story." He expressed confidence he would be back soon. He spoke slowly, his hands clasped, nervously, behind his back, giving the picture of anyone but a "labor agitator." There was something so soft and unworldly about his tone, so symbolic of victims. It was ironic that those who applauded and encouraged him, and who, themselves, had never defied authority in the workplace, nor shared in the sacrifices that are exacted from those who do, were, somehow, so much more sophisticated and had such superior understanding of the absolute powers of management.

On an unparliamentary motion from the self-elected chairman of the meeting, a collection was taken up "to help Chico pay his bills." This was tangible proof of their support—three hundred dollars—and an implied rebuke to the union for denying Chico financial aid.

It became extremely embarrassing to the local union officers that their role in Chico's discharge was being doubted, and that there was gossip in Chico's department that the union wasn't fighting vigorously for his reinstatement.

Chico was called for a conference at the local union office. There he was told about "enemies of our union throwing around a lot of propaganda." The union believes, he was told, that if he wanted his job back, the international union could work it out. They had heard that if he agreed to a one week discipline, and took himself off the contracting-out committee ("it's a useless committee, anyhow") "the company would go along."

Chico asked for time to think it over.

The next day he returned and gave his answer, "I can't sell out my mind!"

The complexities of collective bargaining were patiently explained to Chico, that in a knock-down, drag-out fight with the company, both parties lose, that there must be give and take. "You're listening to a bunch of agitators out there who don't give a god-damn about you. All they're interested in is the next union election."

Again Chico shook his head. "I wish it were all over. I need to get back into the mill. But I can't sell out my mind. With something like this on my record, I'll always be one step from the gate-house."

He insisted he would win his case in arbitration, and that the union couldn't afford to give up a discharge for union activities.

There was no persuading him, and the international union, feeling the pressures within the local union, and the support for Chico among the members, decided to appeal Chico's discharge to arbitration. It was also decided that the international union *would not, would not* charge the company with discrimination on the basis of Chico's union activity or minority status. This was much too delicate a matter. Hard to prove. Opens up the basic assumptions of union-company relations. It's war, and Pittsburgh isn't inclined to go to war with the steel corporations at a time when they are having such successful negotiations. No, it would not be an Article Three Section One case, *(Discrimination Against Any Employee For Union Activity)* nor an Article Three Section Four case, *(Discrimination With Regard to Race, Color, National Origin. . .)* It will have to be an Article Fifteen case *(The Company's Right to Hire, Suspend or Discharge for Proper Cause)*. In arbitration, the charges must be just so, specific to a fault, the exact section of the contract claimed to have been violated must be cited, and there's no changing, adding, or cancelling. If, in the course of the hearing, it became obvious that the aggrieved worker was a victim of discrimination for union activities, or had been deprived of other contractual rights, but that the union had failed to make the charge prior to the hearing, sorry, it's too bad! "An arbitration hearing isn't a fishing expedition," is an abiding principle of labor arbitrators. The union, in Chico's grievance, decided to charge only that there was no "proper cause" for the discharge. Period. "Without an eye-witness," reasoned the union staffman, "the company will have a tough time proving its case." Of course, Chico had no witness either, and though he was skeptical of the union's strategy, it was out of his control.

Walking into the *Towne and Country Motel* conference room where the hearing was scheduled, one was immediately hit by the grimness of the setting. It was strangely like walking into a medieval tribunal. The celebrated round table, symbolizing co-equals in collective bargaining, was never a fixture of arbitration hearings. The company people, (industrial relations personnel, the attorney for the corporation, the superintendent that fired him, Chico's own weld-shop foreman, the plant protection guard who escorted him from the plant) a dozen, in all, were seated at one side of the long rectangular table, and on the other side were the union people (the international union staffman, the local union grievance chairman, and Chico). The arbitrator, regally impartial, sat at the head of the table. Chico was present only as a "witness"—a minor figure in the proceedings. The witness remains in the hearing only for the time required to give testimony and answer to questioning, and then, unless it is mutually agreed that the witness may remain, is excused from the hearing. That's what the union contract provides. Other witnesses may be called up during the course of the hearing, but remaining for the entire hearing is a privilege, a concession, a friendly gesture io a vic tim.

Although it is, in so many ways, a matter of life and death for a worker facing discharge, an arbitration hearing, unlike a civil or criminal court trial in the United States, has absolutely no public character. There is no newspaper or television coverage, no possible review or appeal from a higher body, no protection of a workers job under the due process clause of the United States constitution, no case-law or precedent-binding opinions that an arbitrator must observe, no forum for the rebuttal of the arbitrator's decision. An international union staffman who made a public criticism of a labor arbitrator's decision would be in serious trouble at international headquarters.

It was Chico's first and only experience attending an arbitration hearing, and though he couldn't have been aware of such missing elements as the usual, self-conscious, banter about the stale coffee and sweet rolls provided by the motel management, or the sexist gags about the measurements of the chambermaid who spaced the ashtrays and drew the drapes, he was greatly disturbed by an intuitive sense that he didn't belong there, that he was in a foreign country that spoke a strange language. How was it possible for a working-man or woman to get sucked into such a mire? Maybe generals, senators, governors, mayors, superintendents might consider it worth being subjected to such indignities in exchange for their special privileges. But what special privileges are granted a worker that he or she should agree to face an inquisition? Is working in a steel mill such an exalted position in life? The company should be thankful it can get workers to take all that heat and gas and noise! And who is this arbitrator, anyhow? What qualifies him? Who elected him? Under what shining star was he born?

The hearing, scheduled for nine o'clock in the morning, was delayed an hour, while the company people were closeted in a huddle, apparently working out a strategy, or, as Chico hopefully imagined, were considering dropping the entire matter. He had been told such last-minute maneuvers were not infrequent. The arbitrator, looking at his watch, called the hearing to order. He was a short, middle-aged man with a fleshy face, touched up hair that grew in curls over his ears, dressed in semi-hip clothes that might have become one slimmer and younger. He resembled so many lawyers one saw crowded in the elevators of the Federal Building every morning. The union staffman told Chico he had never laid eyes on him before, but had heard he was formerly a commissioner in the

Michigan labor department, and the permanent arbitrator had recently added him to his staff—a prerogative the union and the corporation had consented to at the time of the signing of the union contract.

In proper form for discharge cases, the company was first in presenting its argument to justify its action, to show that it had acted properly under Article Fifteen of the contract which gives management the right to "suspend or discharge for proper cause." First to testify was the "assaulted" superintendent, the man who fled the mill, bleeding, and sought first aid in the industrial relations office rather than the company hospital. His story was the same he had given in all the previous steps of the grievance procedure, except for the additional information that he had been absent from his plant duties for three weeks, convalescing. (Workers in the plant had been told he was on vacation. There were also rumors he was being transferred to another plant, in Ohio.) An unprovoked attack on a superintendent was certainly "proper cause" for discharge, and the superintendent's account left no room for doubt.

There followed, as a company witness, one of the industrial relations counselors. He told how he had met with the superintendent immediately after the encounter, and had gone with him to the area and taken a number of photographs, which he presented to the arbitrator. Exhibit "A" showed the superintendent's face, with band-aids attached to the nose, forehead, and jaw. Exhibit "B" were photographs of the area where the scuffle took place, showing that it was almost immaculately clean, free from any debris, and no possibility of slipping or tripping, contrary to the union's claim.

Then another spokesman for industrial relations read from a document encased in a manila folder, claiming it was a police report, and giving the impression it came from God's hand, that said Chico had been arrested some three years before for assault, and commented that "Chico has a habit of using his fists," and then limply closed the folder. This was Exhibit "C".

Next the plant-protection guard that escorted Chico from the plant made the point that Chico had offered no protest, no resistance, asked no questions, and appeared satisfied the guard was acting properly.

Then came the "surprise witness." The company presented the superintendent of the outside company which had contracted the fabrication of the furnace skids. He was in the plant that day, he said, and had seen Chico punch his superintendent in the face, knock him to the floor, and kick him several times in the head.

There was no way of knowing how much of the company's case was accepted as truth by the arbitrator, but Chico, less assured than before, audibly whispered to the staffman, "What a bunch of bullshit!" The staffman appeared shaken and uneasy. The arbitrator didn't move a muscle. The company people glanced at one another, chummy and discreetly jubilant.

There is a strange quality to an arbitration hearing in a labor dispute, as if suddenly the workplace has become conscious of its own subtle despotism, and the giant gap between worker and management asserts itself through the thin surface of egalitarianism. The company's cause before the labor arbitrator was so professionally and exhaustively laid out, as if it were a corporate board meeting or a congressional hearing, with an elaborate display of articulate witnesses, neatly typewritten documents, tables, records, charts, photographs, exhibits, all so easily available to management. In contrast, the union side, no matter how much it has tried to imitate big business, was dismally lined up, with only a few, desolate, people on hand, as if nobody in their right mind would care to identify with their cause, amateurs, under-dogs, blue collar workers, over-powered from the very start.

The union staffman was shrewd enough to realize that the "over-kill" strategy of the company had a more ominous goal than getting rid of Chico. It became apparent that the company's intention was to teach the union staffman a lesson in collective bargaining, and he, as much as, or possibly more than

Chico, had become the target of the company's attack. He had previously turned down a company offer to compromise on Chico's discharge, because of the pressures from the local union, especially from Chico's own shopmates in the weld-shop, and he was uneasy about the declining influence of himself and the union in the plant. He wondered, as he watched the company's steady attack, whether he hadn't been too careless.

The staffman, in the conspicuously novel role of a confederate in the arbitration proceedings, shed his usual amiable manners of Labor-Management co-partnership and began earnestly cross-examining the company's witnesses. First, the contractor, the "surprise witness." Why hadn't he made a move to come to the aid of his friend whom he claimed he saw being punched and kicked? Smugly, he answered that he didn't think it would be "proper" for him to interfere in another company's altercations with its employees. Why, then, was he now interfering? Because he believed it was "proper!"

Arbitration, like other professions or trades, has its own distinctive jargon. Acts are described as "proper" or "appropriate" or "reasonable", and there are other such sanctimonious expressions that cover up more than they explain, and have, over the years, fixed the tone and temper of collective bargaining. The words are always the same. Only the time and the place seem to change.

The union staffman, not being trained as an attorney, and suddenly become aware that the rules and the grammar of arbitration had changed, probably did the best he could. It was one thing to cross-examine an outside contractor-superintendent he had never seen before, but something quite different when face to face with the plant officials he had been successfully dealing with over a number of years. He had learned early in his profession never to corner a tiger. The mill superintendent, when questioned, didn't explain why, if bleeding and bruised, he went to the industrial relations office rather than the plant dispensary, except that he thought it was the "proper" course to take. It would appear that the next question would be "You weren't really hurt that much, were you?" But it wasn't asked.

Next, the plant guard who had escorted Chico from the plant, made a big point that Chico hadn't resisted or protested, implying a consciousness of guilt. What kind of protest would it have been "appropriate" for Chico to make? That wasn't for him to say.

The physical appearance of the area in front of the furnace was in dispute. A witness for Chico had testified it was cluttered with mill scrap and debris and that photos displayed at the hearing were false, probably touched up. The company attorney, poised and unhurried, called for a ten minute recess to call one of their foremen from the plant as a witness. The foreman arrived, frightened and puffing, and, other than that he was expected to bolster the company's argument in arbitration, didn't know for what specific purpose he had been called. He was immediately sworn in (the company insisted, in this case, that all its witnesses be sworn, though it isn't required or customary) and he identified himself as a millwright foreman in the thirty-two inch mill. Then he responded to questions from the company lawyer. He was obviously confused. Or he could have decided to take his oath seriously.

Did you have occasion to pass by the furnace area on the day of the incident with Chico?

Yes, several times. The furnace repairs were part of my duties.

Did you see the encounter between Chico and the superintendent?

No.

Look at these photographs. Do they look like the area in front of the furnace?

No. Not on that day. It was a repair turn, and my men were piling scrap metal, discarded machine parts, old tubing and other junk on the floor in 'D' Bay near the furnace. I had it all carried away the next day.

In a spectacular murder trial, in the days of the extra edition, that would have been the point when the newsmen would have rushed to the telephones to give their editors the sensational headline. But the company reacted more casually. It asked for another ten minute recess.

It was again rumored that during the recess the industrial relations people pressed the mill officials to make another offer to the union—for a settlement of the case without completing the arbitration hearing. Such procedure is "legitimate" and frequently occurs. But the mill superintendent balked. Claimed it would ruin his reputation in the mill. "And, furthermore, I want that millwright foreman fired. Today!"

The hearing reconvened and Chico gave his version of the events of that day.

The arbitrator asked Chico why he hadn't complained or protested when the plant guards came for him. "To whom should I have complained? There's no set-up in the plant for protesting the activities of plant protection. I had to do what he asked. He had a gun."

When nobody knew what more questions to ask, or whom to call up as another witness—if only somebody who was believable could be found—the hearing finally ended.

Everyone walked out of the conference room of the *Towne and Country Motel,* the witnesses, supervisors, industrial relations counselors, stenographers, union people, the arbitrator, all slightly dazed, drained of sensitivity from suffering through an all-day performance without style, without elegance, without subtlety, without sincerity. It stank, but no one could walk out on it before the final curtain.

Chico asked the union staffman: How do you think we did?

He answered with a shrug of his shoulder: It's your word against the word of two superintendents.

Two weeks later the arbitrator's decision arrived.

The discharge was *sustained.*

Chapter Twelve

Is There a Doctor in the Workplace?

Charlie Shannon had a fluke accident in "C" Bay, when he discovered, too late, that the electric transfer car he was operating had no brakes, and he had to jump off before it hit the wall of wooden ties set up for such emergencies. He fell backwards and landed against a pile-up of cold steel sitting along the track. It took away his breath for a moment, and he felt a pain in his chest. He went to the plant dispensary, as all employees are exhorted to do in case of injury in the plant, and the plant nurse recorded the accident, where, how and when it happened, the particulars of Charlie's physical complaints, when he had last attended a safety meeting, who his foreman was, and told him to wait for Dr. Small for possible X-rays.

Dr. Small had more seniority at Republic Steel than anyone in the plant, worker or supervisor. Works managers, industrial relations superintendents, operational supervision come and go, but Dr. Small's post as chief medical doctor in the plant remained fixed, as if welded to its truss. It was rumored that he was one of the corporation's big stockholders, and was an important figure in the Cleveland main office. His own medical office on Exchange Street, in South Chicago, was one of the few centers in the city where one could browse through Billy James Hargis' radical-right *Weekly Crusader* (there was no other publication in his waiting room) and acquire privileged information on how to save America from a liberal-communist take-over. (Incidentally, this Billy James was the same creep who later, in 1976, became notorious as an exposed male-child molester in Oklahoma.) To what extent the corporation identified with the strange doctrines of Billy James, nobody can positively know. But there is documentary evidence (published in the book *Danger on the Right*) that Republic Steel corporation gave large financial contributions to the far-right wing National Education Program, which had inter-locking ties with the Reverend Billy James Hargis and the John Birch Society.

That there is something in a person's politics or philosophy that clings to his working profession cannot be disproved. But how, in Dr. Small's case, it really influenced his practice of medicine cannot be sworn to. Except that few workers at the plant would disagree that Dr. Small's diagnoses often fitted the company's economic interests rather than the worker's state of health.

Charlie, waiting in the dispensary, holding his hand to his chest to ease the pain, knew nothing and cared less about these subtle and obscure influences in Dr. Small's career. But there were some serious incidents between the doctor and the workers in the plant which had become matters of record.

For example, when the doctor examined Bill Fenderson, a mill operator who blacked out while on the job, he diagnosed it as "due to high blood pressure," and ruled Fenderson unfit for any work in the plant. He had that power. Whereupon, the company terminated Fenderson.

Fenderson had fourteen years in the plant, and under the union contract in force at that time, it was necessary to work fifteen years to qualify for a company pension due to disability. He was short one year. If Fenderson were let go he would have got nothing from the plant—no pension, no insurance, no severance pay, and only the slimmest chance for a job in some other plant. There had been instances where employees were fired just before they would have become eligible for a pension, but the case of Fenderson was just too much.

He had been "chewed out" several times in the past for having slowed down production—not willfully, but he just didn't seem able to keep up, to get in that extra motion. It was true. He wasn't as quick and didn't have the stamina as some of the others who were ten or fifteen years younger. The mistake was that, at his age, he probably shouldn't have been hired into the mill crew. Not that it was like an assembly line where each operation was timed. But a rolling mill crew pushes itself hard to get out the tonnage and thus build up its incentive earnings. One poky operator can make an awful hole in the incentive pay. However, even the most money-hungry member of the crew, if consulted, would have flatly opposed firing Fenderson on such grounds. They might have gone along with changing him to another job that wasn't so critical, but firing him was a disgustingly unfair solution. Neither did they go along with what looked so much like a company con-game in finding Fenderson unfit for work. Workers in the plant always suspected the plant dispensary to be an adjunct of the personnel department, ready to do its bidding, capable of any dirty trick. It always seemed too aggressive, too mighty, too cold-blooded, too much an intrusion into their private lives. This mistrust is highlighted yearly, during the period of physical examinations that all employees are required to take. It's a routine examination that takes no more than a few minutes—blood pressure, a couple of taps on the chest, the classical hernia cough, a trip to the scale, not worth a plugged nickel—and one might be puzzled why workers try to avoid this yearly physical, why the nervousness and anxiety. It goes much beyond workers' historical aversion to surrendering defenselessly to the insolent scrutiny of upper class professionals. Workers with undiagnosed symptoms dread that that could be the day the plant doctor might do them in and declare them physically unfit for further employment.

The Fenderson medical discharge is cited as a clear-cut example, because when Fenderson's local union grievanceman produced the letter from the family physician stating that Fenderson was being treated by him for the flu, and that his past medical history showed *low* blood pressure, Dr. Small and the company hastily retreated, and Fenderson was restored to his job. But it started lively speculation in the plant whether the plant doctor even had a license to practice medicine.

Charlie told Dr. Small how he had fallen when he jumped off the transfer car, and where he was hurting. The doctor read from the record the nurse had written, and, not quite looking at him, asked, "what's your trouble, son?"

"I guess I got hurt. I have a bad pain in my chest."

Still avoiding him, the doctor asked Charlie to remove his shirt. Then he told him to step on the scale. "You're too light for your job," and without examining him any further the doctor told him to put his shirt back on and to ask his foreman that he be put on "light duty." (Charlie was a motor inspector, which, according to the job description manual, required "moderate physical exertion," and he knew of no way the job could be done on light duty.)

He returned to his shop, and with the generous help of the other motor inspectors, managed to get through the day. On his way out of the mill he stopped again to see the plant doctor. He told him again he had "bad pains in the chest." This time Dr. Small looked up angrily, and shouted, that those pains are a heart condition. The company doesn't treat heart conditions or any diseases. Only accidents on the job. (Plant dispensaries, by character and convention, are not oriented or equipped to deal with a worker who is stricken. Plant dispensaries function principally to protect the plant, rather than the worker.)

When Charlie got home, the pains got worse, and he went to his family doctor. An X-ray showed two cracked ribs, and he was immediately sent to South Chicago community hospital. He was in bed less than an hour when he had visitors—his foreman, the superintendent of the electrical department, and the safety engineer from the plant.

Charlie was startled, and he couldn't for the life of him figure out what he had done to warrant such attention. Could he have left his safety lock on a piece of equipment and they are after the key? Or are they going to hand him a discipline slip —maybe give him time off? Here he was, in pain and drained of strength, and they're still on his back. Didn't he have the right to be left alone in a hospital bed?

But the supervisors were surprisingly warm and friendly. They told him they were sorry he got hurt, and that the brakes on the transfer car had been repaired. They asked him if there was anything they could do for him. Did he want any cigarettes or magazines? Charlie thanked them and said he didn't need anything, and appreciated their coming to see him. Did he want them to call his wife? No, thanks, she would be visiting him later. The safety superintendent then explained that all employees operating the transfer car should first check out the brakes, which Charlie, in his state of mind, interpreted as a personal reproach, and again caused him to wonder what they were really after. It didn't take long to find out. Charlie's superintendent came to the point. Nobody, of course, took notes, and these were the words recalled from memory, several weeks later, after Charlie returned to work:

We talked to your doctor and he says it'll take two or three weeks for your ribs to heal. There's no medicine or bandaging that can help. Just rest. No physical exertion, no twisting or lifting. Just rest. You know you don't have to be cooped up here in the hospital. They're not going to help you. You can do just as well, better, resting in the electric shop. We can have you picked up every morning at your home and drive you directly to the plant. Read fuck-books, magazines, do crossword puzzles, do whatever you want, but no physical work. If you get bored, you can sort prints or answer the telephone, if you feel like it. You know, if you're punched in every day you'll draw your regular paycheck. What do you get on sick pay? Eighty, ninety dollars? You know you can't live on it. You might just as well get your regular pay. And when you're all knit together, your regular job is here waiting for you.

Then the superintendent swallowed, and cleared his throat, and Charlie knew he was coming to the real heart of the matter: We'd hate to see our department charged with a *lost-time accident.* (*Lost-time accident* is a strange term, that gives no clue to the extent of the injuries, the amount of suffering, which, or how many, limbs are damaged, the extent of the disability. It's a term for an industrial accident that results in the worker being absent from the job one or more days. If the injured worker reports on his next scheduled work day, it's no lost-time accident. Industry, government, insurance underwriters, safety councils, employer associations, compile statistics and publish reports on this highly sensitive industrial problem, and these are used as arguments for or against legislation, workmen's compensation schedules, safety regulations, and in persuading the public that, indeed, as the National Association of Manufacturers has always said, and as is devotedly repeated at thousands of monthly safety meetings in the workplaces throughout the land, "the average American is safer in the workplace than he is at home.")

The superintendent, shifting in his chair, pitifully uncomfortable, murmured that it would be shameful to have a lost-time accident. Why? Nobody gains from it. It'd be different if they could do something in the hospital about those ribs. All the doctors agree. No need to stay in the hospital. He offered to drive him home, and a taxicab would pick him up in the morning and drive him to the plant.

Charlie knew the superintendent was right. His own doctor told him there was no treatment except rest, and in three or four weeks he'd be well. If the company was willing to have him lay around the shop and pay him full wages, why should he object? But why didn't Dr. Small tell him the truth? That heart-disease story was enough to scare a man half to death. Son-of-a-bitch!

Charlie remained silent, trying to find an answer. A nurse came in with papers for him to sign, and seeing him hesitate, the superintendent offered another plan. That he remain in the hospital another day, and his foreman would change his work-schedule to show it was a day "off", as if he were on a four-day week, and then when he punched in the next morning there would be no record, absolutely no record of a lost-time day. Thus, outdoing the alchemists who dreamed of turning lead into gold, with a flick of the foreman's pencil, a lost-time accident can be totally converted into a non-accident.

That non-work day arranged for Charlie's benefit gave him a chance to think. He knew he was miserable and there was only one medicine that would make him well and ease every inch of his pain. He rang for the nurse, and told her he didn't want any of those people from the steel company visiting him. Nobody, except his wife.

The next day he went home. He stayed home and sat around for three solid weeks, twenty-one days, to give his ribs a chance to mend, doing the best he could on company sick-pay. He said he had never felt so healthy and happy in all his life.

Before returning to work, he was required, under the company rules, to undergo a physical examination by the company doctor. It's more a clerical check than a medical one, and the workers regard it as further company intrusion into their private lives. Dr. Small, not one to hold a personal grudge or to stray from company policy, placed his hand on Charlie's chest, as a faith-healer might, smiled self-consciously, and said, "I'd have sworn you had a heart condition," and fixed his signature on the company form for a return to work.

If this were the close of this pitifully vulgar affair between a steelworker who had the misfortune of a lost-time accident and a company typically committed to the invalidation of all such accidents, it would tell enough about the extensive concealment of unsafe conditions and the wretched status of medical attention in the workplaces of America. But, of course, there was more.

Mesmerized by its own official accounts, the company continued to blank out the fact that Charlie had a lost-time accident, and, instead of providing state workmen's compensation, as is due a worker incapacitated by an industrial accident, the company provided the regular sick pay due any worker in the plant who is sick for more than one week and is off from work. In either kind of compensation the amount is the same. But Charlie, now on guard, didn't like the smell of it. He had no stomach for participating, after all that had happened, in a slick company scheme to hush up a lost-time accident. He insisted his accident-pay must come from state workmen's compensation.

He returned the sick-pay checks to the company, without cashing them. Several months later—eight months, to be exact—the company settled Charlie's workmen's compensation claim, and he received full payment for the entire three weeks he was off, and he filed another claim for a lump sum payment, as the workmen's compensation law provides in the event of broken ribs in a job-related accident. Then, and only then, did it become a fact that Charlie had cracked a couple of ribs in a lost-time accident on a transfer car that had defective brakes. It should cause anyone to be wary of the slogan that "the average American is safer in the workplace than he is at home."

Chapter Thirteen

The Blue Collar Apprentice—
an Endangered Species

When Ziggy applied at the employment office of Republic Steel in 1969, he had just turned eighteen and he told them he wanted to learn a trade, like a machinist or electrician. He said he wanted to start as an apprentice and work his way up.

His father had told him many times that if you have a skilled trade you will never be out of a job. Even in the depression a good mechanic didn't have to worry. And how many times he had been told that the trouble in this country was that workers had "no pride in their work!" Ziggy decided he wanted to begin his work career on the right path.

The employment office recognized that here was an admirable worker, much superior to the type pouring in from the South at that time, and advised Ziggy there were no openings for apprentices in the plant at the moment, but he would do well to hire in as an "oiler" in the mechanical department, and he could easily work his way up to a "millwright" in a year or two. That's a good trade, and doesn't require an apprenticeship, and it pays the same as a machinist or electrician. And, if an apprenticeship opened up later on, and he was still interested in it, he would have the opportunity to transfer. We'll let you know when there's an opening.

Ziggy thought that was sensible and decent of him, and he hired in as an oiler in the mechanical department, and was assigned to one of the rolling mills.

About six months later, it was after he had been on his long weekend, Ziggy learned, quite by accident, that a new man was hired to fill an apprenticeship in the electrical trade. Before his long weekend he checked in at the employment office, as was his regular routine, to inquire if there was an apprenticeship opening, and the answer was no, we will notify you if there is.

Ziggy had already been promoted from oiler to millwright helper, a job he liked, but the thought of an apprenticeship and learning a regular trade never left him. The success stories, told by his father, of skilled tradesmen in the Great Depression, became more vivid with time.

Ziggy was in the locker-room, changing into his work-clothes that morning, and a young man he didn't recognize sat down beside him and began unpacking his shopping bag. It contained a denim shirt with the pins still in, work jeans right out of the Army-Navy store, a spanking new pair of metatarsal safety shoes, a shiny brown, plastic, hard-hat, and a pair of unspeckled safety-goggles—all the symptoms of a newly hired employee. They talked and he discovered they had been students together at St. Francis de Sales High, and he had just graduated. That morning he had been hired as an apprentice in the electric shop. Ziggy asked him to repeat. Yes, it was an apprenticeship in the electric shop.

The blood drained from Ziggy's face. He no longer wanted to talk or listen. He had been double-crossed and this punk kid who probably has an uncle in the front office knows a lot more than he's telling.

Ziggy went to the shop and told his foreman what had happened. The foreman said it was tough titty, and then, more sympathetically, confessed that he himself had once apprenticed in the machine shop, but unless you're going for supervision, you're a hell-of-a-lot better off in what you're doing. In a couple of years you'll be a millwright, and that skinny punk apprentice will still be a skinny punk apprentice running for coffee and sweeping the shop.

He let the matter ride for a few days, but the hurting didn't let up. He dropped by the employment office and there he was told that it was the first that office had heard of it. He must've been "hired direct," was as specific as they'd get.

Advised by his union grievanceman, he filed a grievance charging the company with violating his rights to become an apprentice.

At the risk of furnishing more information than most people care to have about apprenticeship, but, on the other hand, in order to fully explain Ziggy's grievance and the tremors it evoked in the plant, some keys must be provided to place the institution of apprenticeship in its proper slot, and to separate the mythological from the real world of apprenticeship.

In most workplaces, in the United States, except on building and construction, the blue collar workers doing the higher-skilled and higher-paid jobs are not recruited, as is commonly believed, from industry-sponsored and union-supported apprenticeship programs. Only a tiny fragment of today's skilled blue collar workers travels that formal road. The overwhelming majority are hired off the streets into the bottom jobs of the workplace, and are then promoted, step by step, into the more skilled, and finally into the most highly skilled jobs and occupations. The promotions in unionized shops, most simply stated, are based on length of service in the plant, ability, and physical fitness. Even in non-union plants, where other compelling factors are absent—family, race, pay-ola, clout—these are the qualifications for promotion. Apprenticeship is hardly in the picture. Apprenticeship has given way to on-the-job training in both unionized and non-union workplaces.

(The building and construction industry continues to hang on to apprenticeship training for reasons hardly related to the mastering of work skills. These will be explored a bit later.)

It's not only the highly-skilled production jobs in industry, such as rollers, or melters, or heaters, in the steel industry, or the comparable production jobs in other industries, that are filled without benefit of apprenticeship. But craft jobs, too, the kind of jobs we have always been told require a rigorous four or five year apprenticeship, including one day a week in trade schools, and a couple of relatives in the union office, are now filled, for the most part, (except in the building and construction industry) by workers who start as helpers, pick up skills, and climb the promotional ladder to become boilermakers, millwrights, welders, carpenters, riggers, blacksmiths. Pay scales for craftsmen in industry are considerably lower than for the building and construction workers. A craftsman in a steel mill or automobile plant or refinery often works side by side with a craftsman who is in the plant on a temporary basis as an employee of a construction company doing repairs, and the plant employee is paid three or four dollars an hour less than the outside craftsman employed by a construction contractor.

Corporate industry, while conceding to apprenticeship in the building trades, is successfully destroying it in all other employment.

The 1973 annual report of Chicago's Danly Machine Corporation deplored "the very adverse effect on our gross margins (of profit) in training new personnel" and a spokesman for the corporation bluntly announced its curtailment of future apprenticeship and training programs.

George Morris, a General Motors Corporation vice-president, said, at a 1972 meeting of the Construction Users Anti-Inflation Roundtable: "We have building trade union members rubbing shoulders with our own auto workers union skilled mechanics who perform the same jobs. The building trades people are not above saying, 'Hey, buddy. If you were a member of the electrical workers union instead of the auto workers, you'd have this kind of paycheck.' "

The skilled tradesmen in the auto workers union, attempting to close the pay-gap, have won the theoretical right to veto all union contracts, but haven't succeeded in coming near the wage scales of the skilled building and construction tradesmen.

A spokesman for the Tool and Die Institute in the Chicago area, Mike Lane, approaching the problem from another angle, complained that, "In his second year an apprentice toolmaker is making $4 or $5 an hour, and all of a sudden he gets a chance to take a job as a truck driver at 50 cents an hour more, and we lose him."

The AFL-CIO, unruffled by the systematic decline in industrial apprenticeship, in its August 1975 issue of the *American Federationist,* reported 250,000 Americans currently enrolled in formal apprenticeship programs in the various trades. Accepting these figures, and brushing aside that the overwhelming enrollment of apprentices are from the very, very special category of building and construction trades, they confirm statistically what every worker plainly sees: that less than one-half of one percent of the entire blue collar work force are being trained to become skilled workers by way of apprenticeship. To put it into perspective, to underline the crumbling of a system, a comparison with the system in the legal or medical profession is relevant.

With 325,000 lawyers in the United States *(American Almanac, 1975),* there are roughly 100,000 students in law and pre-law schools preparing for the profession. There are 130,-000 students in pre-medical and medical colleges training for a profession that has 330,000 licensed physicians. In both cases a proportion of better than one trainee for every three licensed professionals. Granted that blue collar worker's skills don't precisely fit the circumstances of professional practitioners, and that all students in law or medical schools don't necessarily graduate, this vast discrepancy shows how thoroughly the work process in blue collar industry has been down-graded and regimented since the days of Frederick

Winslow Taylor's *Principles of Scientific Management,* and helps to ascribe responsibility for this lack of "pride in our work" we hear so much about.

The vestiges of apprenticeship programs that still survive in the workplace are maintained artificially and synthetically. They represent a cultural lag, habit, or are for purposes of industrial morale or pride, but, more often, *as a source for supervisory personnel.* Workers in the plant have a keen sense that those who are selected for the limited openings for apprenticeships have somehow already been tapped for a boss' job. A blue collar worker, now-a-days, without ambition to enter supervision, doesn't bother to apply. It is remarkable how many group leaders, foremen and superintendents in industry have arrived by way of craft apprenticeship. Even young men with college degrees are frequently assigned to apprenticeships as their first job.

Not altogether irrelevant is the preponderant number of former apprentices and craftsmen who become union officers —both local unions and international boards—in the production industries as well as the building and construction. Although there are other valid reasons why workers on production jobs, on shift-work, or under assembly-line conditions, restricted to a small area of the plant, find it more difficult than skilled workers do, to be active in the affairs of their local union, the influence industry can and does exert in determining and shaping union leadership is of much greater substance than has been generally perceived.

Except for disclosures of outright bribery, or for doctrinaire denunciations of union leaders as "agents of the bosses," there has been all too little study of the subtle mechanisms through which industry has forwarded the selection of international leadership of unions—local unions, too—in the United States. Indeed, there has been, of late, greater disclosures of the manner in which the union leaderships in Chile and other Latin-American countries have been manipulated by American corporate interests than of its manipulation of AFL-CIO leaderships.

(To cite a quite unnoticed regular local union election for office at Republic Steel plant in South Chicago, one of the candidates for president of Local 1033 was Gus, a journeyman machinist, first class. A year before the election, the company created a new job, that of a "grinding wheel inspector," and assigned Gus to fill the job. The duties were to measure with a rule the size of grinding wheels on various machines throughout the plant. There had never been such a job in the plant, and if there were need for such, it could easily have been filled by one with less skill than a first class machinist. The job quietly disappeared after the local union election. But for that one year Gus was given the rare opportunity to walk all over the sprawling plant, from department to department, to conduct a person-to-person campaign for president of the local union. There was no foreman to warn him about doing "union business on company time" or any limits to where to travel, no fear of being charged with "being away from his work area," as other candidates might, and did encounter. Needless to say, Gus was elected president.)

Among the most popularly known facts of the American labor movement is that George Meany was a plumber, and that Jimmy Hoffa was a truck driver. Not quite so well known is that Walter Reuther and I.W. Abel also came from the *crafts* (machinists). Search the leadership of the unions of America, industrial as well as craft unions, affiliated as well as independent unions, "left-wing" as well as "right-wing", and one is struck by the small number of leading officials who come from the ranks of industrial production. Again, take the steel industry, as an example. The craft workers there are a tiny minority. But craftsmen predominate as local union presidents, and, insofar as they have any industry background at all, district directors and international officers also come from the crafts. Such big steel union locals as Inland Steel, U.S.

Steel in Chicago and in Gary, Republic Steel, Youngstown Sheet and Tube, have almost never elected a production worker as their president.

The decline and fall of apprenticeship had been forecasted in 1776 by Adam Smith. He wrote, truly enough, in the *Wealth of Nations:* "Long apprenticeships are altogether unnecessary. The arts, which are much superior to common trades, such as those making clocks and watches, contain no such mystery as to require a long course of instruction. The first invention of such beautiful machines, indeed, even that of some of the instruments employed in making them, must, no doubt, have been the work of deep thought and long time, and may justly be considered as among the happiest efforts of human ingenuity. But when both have been fairly invented and well understood, to explain to any young man, in the completest manner, how to apply the instruments and how to construct the machines, cannot well require more than the lessons of a few weeks . . . ".

Adam Smith's crystal ball might easily have been registering a close-up of the present day glazier's apprenticeship. During the first year, the glazier apprentice is not permitted to go up a ladder or perform any work handling glass. He may only mix putty, carry the ladder, and perform menial and unskilled tasks related to the craft. After one full year of apprenticeship he is no more qualified to place a window-light into a frame than any other self-trained do-it-yourself homeowner. For two additional years the glazier-apprentice is restrained from performing any significant work in the trade, unless a sudden shortage of labor were to develop. Similar restrictions predominate in practically all apprenticeship programs

Blue collar workers in industry are doing jobs requiring skills and experience equal or superior to the journeyman in any occupation or craft. They begin in the simpler and lower-paid jobs, and advance, usually, without any prescribed restraint on the learning of skills. They perform the full scope of the work on the job they fill. A worker in a manufacturing plant operates a one hundred ton crane, making lifts requiring the utmost skill and precision, quite the same as is required of a crane operator on a construction site. But the plant crane operators are given a "break-in" period of a week or two, on, first, a smaller crane, and then on bigger and still bigger cranes, as the job openings occur, while the operator at the construction site goes through a smug and leisurely four years of unproductive and often humiliating, mickey-mouse course of instruction, before being recognized as a crane operator. Craftsmen who have come to their occupations by the route of apprenticeship, whether crane operator, welder, carpenter, millwright, boilermaker, or any of the scores of trades listed in the United States Department of Labor's *Dictionary of Occupational Titles,* and are members of craft unions affiliated with the Building and Construction Trades Council (AFL-CIO), are paid a higher scale, often as much as double that of members of industrial unions (also affiliated with the AFL-CIO) performing almost identical work in factories and industrial plants as craft workers in the building trades. (This is in no way intended to lend support to the brash charges from anti-labor quarters, or from pinched middle class consumers and exhausted bargain-hunters, that craftsmen's wages are a rip-off. Anyone trying to balance the ten or fifteen dollar an hour scale for the worker who climbs a scaffold to cover a roof or installs an electrical outlet, against the one hundred dollar an hour fee for the dentist who drills a canal, or the lawyer who equivocates in the courtroom, would accomplish little besides catching themselves up in their own class prejudices.)

The building trades worker, being more visible to the public while at work, is better known and is checked out more surely than blue collar workers employed in remote, walled-in workplaces on the city's outskirts, punching in and out at unnatural hours, and hardly ever seen, unless one happens to live in their community. But which suburbanite, on an urban shopping tour, or white collar employee during lunch hour or as a diversion, hasn't assumed the stance of the "sidewalk engineer" beholding the nimble motions of the power shovel-operator or pile-driver erecting a skyscraper or laying a bridge? Or which condominium owner hasn't had a personal to-do with the painter, plumber, washing machine repairman whose employer he or she has fortuitously become? And who in America has escaped the elaborate commercial promotion of the infernal CB radio which has rhapsodized the truck-driver? All in all, in considering the workers in America, most people have a clearer image of the outside craftsmen, than of the blue collar worker inside the mills, factories, shops and mines.

The over-balancing influence and power of the craft unions within the labor movement, except during that brief period of the development of the CIO, has not been seriously challenged by the industrial unions. They have been quite content in their role as junior partners in Labor. But this submission, in itself, cannot account for the unions of the building and construction trades, with about three million members—not overwhelming out of a total of more than twenty million union members—excercising such a monopoly of Labor's influence in politics, foreign policy, national economic policy, and on the White House.

It is almost impossible to adjust one's mind to the disproportionate control enjoyed by the craft unions without taking into account that industry and government entrust these conservative and basically friendly labor unions (themselves conducted like businesses instead of brotherhoods) to conform and align properly and obediently with the goals of business. For this they receive a share of the prize. This isn't a novel accusation. It is routinely levelled by some social critics against all labor unions. However, a conspiracy on that grand a scale is rather hard to swallow, and would be self-destructive. It's too apparent that the big and important deals have been with the craft unions, and the rest of the labor movement got either a bit of the left-overs, or the boot.

The biggest deal, of course, was the craft union's successful obstruction of union organization in the basic industries—the vital centers of the economy. The mass production industries, like steel, auto, chemicals, aluminum, rubber, petroleum, operated for many decades without unions, (except for the thin layer of skilled craftsmen) conferring on those industries such benefits as low pay scales, wretched working conditions, and dictatorial power over its workers. The craft unions were officially recognized, had solid treasuries, staff, and political clout, and would not, under any conditions, admit the production workers into their unions. They actively opposed all efforts to organize them into industrial unions. For this fantastic service rendered to industry, the craft union members received such prizes and benefits as wages higher than other workers, improved working conditions, subsidized and genteel apprenticeship for their kinfolk, union control of the jobs and the title of "aristocrats of Labor." The leaders of these craft unions controlled their members like no other organization, by reason of their influence with industry and government. The craftsman's livelihood depended entirely upon the union. (Some irreverent students of Labor have hinted that these special rewards constitute a form of bribery and corruption—an idea first suggested by Karl Marx in reference to the British trade union support for British imperialism and colonial aggression.)

The set-back delivered the craft unions with the enactment of the Wagner labor law by the Roosevelt administration, and the formation of the Congress for Industrial Organization (CIO) in 1935, was only temporary. The building trades unions regained a mightier position in the nation as the dominating force in a *merged* AFL-CIO, giving the expanded labor movement its distinct business-like style and program. The business community was almost unanimous in praise of the merger, after it had slowly destroyed the CIO with the Taft-Hartley law, McCarthyism, and witch-hunts.

Among other services and courtesies the craft unions leadership extended to the establishment, extremely important and sensitive were the covert activities in behalf of the CIA and the State Department, and their joint sponsorship with corporate interests of the American Institute for Free Labor Development (AIFLD) to extend American political and business influence in Latin America. (This was one of the chief complaints of the Auto Workers Union in disaffiliating from the AFL-CIO. However, several industrial unions, including the Auto Workers, were drawn into this secret activity.)

When former President Nixon needed blue collar workers to demonstrate in support of the war in Viet Nam, he knew where to go. The building trades unions, during work-time paid for by the contractors, sent its hard-hatted tradesmen to rough up anti-war students. These were unions that could be depended upon. But such loyalty doesn't come cheap!

Such favors to the establishment were duly, and often outrageously, rewarded. In addition to the economic inducements already cited, the unions associated with the building and construction trades received such tangibles and intangibles as:

1. Preferential laws, such as the federal Bacon-Davis Act and the Walsh-Healey Act, and any number of state "mini Bacon-Davis Acts" single out the building and construction unions for special protection, compensation and gratuities. The laws compel construction companies and contractors performing government work (and government contracts employ or influence the employment of the greatest number of construction workers in the United States) to pay the workers the prevailing union scale of wages—a "sweatheart deal" of the first magnitudue. These laws also guarantee that the training and apprenticeship program remain under union control. And, of course, the laws have been effective in excluding Blacks, Latinos and other minorities from the industry.

2. When the federal government, under pressure of the civil rights movement, launched its Manpower Development and Training program to prepare the "hard core" unemployed for jobs, it flatly exempted training for any building and con-

struction jobs. It wasn't about to mess with the "restricted" apprenticeship program of these unions.

3. When the federal Pay Board, in 1971, clamped a ceiling of 5.5 per cent on wage raises, an exception was made for the building and construction workers to allow them 10 to 12 per cent wage increases.

Ironically, and grievously, the building and construction workers, who earn every penny they get, and have only the remotest involvement in the complicated mechanism of industry-union agreements, are viewed by lower-paid and lesser-protected workers as the chief culprits in the "sweatheart deals" which have been so effective in reducing the status of other workers, both organized and unorganized.

4. Foremen in construction and building trades are members of the same union as the workers they supervise (held to be a violation of the labor law for industrial unions) and any rank and file union member who might entertain a notion of running for union office, but doesn't want to have a run-in with his foreman, would best re-consider.

5. Pension and welfare funds for workers in the building trades (and teamsters) are controlled by the union leadership, giving the union members another good incentive to refrain from dissent, and supplying the leadership the use of large sums of money to make business loans and strengthen its own position. Criminally-connected enterprises have been frequent beneficiaries of such loans.

6. The links between the criminal underworld and the leadership of the building trades and the closely-associated teamsters, though quite thoroughly exposed by Congress, and frequently the well-spring of labor violence and assasinations, are, apparently, immune from the enforcement of the law. Employers and contractors, some with close personal ties with union leaders and the crime syndicate, some having previously served as union officials or crime figures, accept this link-up as an agreeable way to do business. While the law has been notoriously hostile to Labor through most of the history of the

labor movement, and especially to union efforts in mass production industry, it has been perversely sympathetic and friendly with the corrupted union organaizations. Tony Boyle, former president of the United Mineworkers, pacing a cell in prison for the assasination of Jock Yablonski (his opponent in a union election) and pondering what he had done wrong, might well reach the conclusion he could have fared better had he been a president in the building trades or teamsters union.

The future of apprenticeship is not likely to become the subject of great internal debate within the top circles of the trade unions, nor of industry, and government. Except for the larger question of how much voice the rank and file of labor will be able to command in making decisions on the nature and conditions of work, the matter of apprenticeship is settled.

But not entirely for Ziggy, whose grievance has been left dangling in the first step of the collective bargaining procedure at Republic Steel in South Chicago.

If the grievance accomplished nothing else, it opened up questions about apprenticeship that nobody had recently thought about.

This is how the grievance looked written on its proper form (the first paragraph is the official, contractual, language, printed at the top of the grievance papers in atrociously unreadable, six point, bold, type; the other paragraphs were filled in by Ziggy's grievanceman):

REPUBLIC STEEL CORPORATION GRIEVANCE FORM

Subject to the provisions of the Labor Agreement, I hereby authorize the representative of the Union which is recognized by the Company as my collective bargaining agent to process this request or claim arising therefrom in this or any other step of the grievance procedure, including arbitration, or to adjust or settle the same.

STATEMENT OF GRIEVANCE: *Zigmont Gorski, an oiler in the mechanical department, protests that a new hire was assigned an apprenticeship, in violation of the seniority rights of the aggrieved.*

FACTS: *The grievant has greater length of service than the incumbent apprentice. He has the physical fitness and the ability to perform the job. The apprenticeship was not posted, as other jobs are, denying the grievant the opportunity to bid on the vacancy.*

REMEDY REQUESTED: *The Union requests that the grievant be assigned to the apprenticeship in the electrical shop which was improperly assigned to an employee of lesser service.*

(Signed) *Zygmont Gorski*
(Employee's Signature)
Charles Spencer
(Union Representative's Signature)

It was, in most respects, a grievance in the pattern of some six hundred other grievances filed by employees in this plant during that year, charging violations of rights. There was one unusual twist. In the thirty-five years of collective bargaining in this plant, and the thousands of grievances filed in those years complaining about company violations of the labor agreement, this was the first ever filed on the subject of apprenticeship. Apprenticeships had always been filled by the Company on any basis it chose. This was strictly a management prerogative, actually under looser regulation than in the Babylonian Empire.

Ziggy's grievance never would have seen the light of day, except for the passage of the Civil Rights Act of 1964 and Title VII of the act. To keep the union contract in line with the new law, but not to encourage any basic changes, the union and the Company added the Memorandum of Understanding on Apprenticeship to the appendices of the contract—the *Appendices,* which, presumably, nobody ever reads: "Apprenticeship vacancies shall be filled on the same basis as other permanent vacancies and shall be subject to the posting practices of the plant." With that done, the Company as before, meticulously brought in the sons and nephews of supervisors whenever an if ever an apprenticeship was to be filled. That is, until Ziggy filed a grievance.

In the Company's eye, Ziggy was completely out of it. If he had thought this thing through he would have known he was out of it, and he wouldn't have filed. If the Company was seeking a skilled hand, it wouldn't start him off as an apprentice. It would start him as a helper or some other bottom job and let him progress as far as his ambitions and talents would take him. That's the way a modern industrial plant builds up its work force.

Appealed to the second step, Industrial Relations, less ruffled than a priest repeating his beads, intoned that the company has "acted properly under Article Ten of the labor agreement." If Ziggy didn't see the notice it was his own fault, because they posted it. And they produced a typewritten notice which they said was the one they posted. The grievance was denied in the second step. In the third step of the grievance procedure, Industrial Relations came up with a list of seven names—employees who they said had responded to the posted notice and had made application to fill the apprenticeship. They took the apprenticeship written test, and, unfortunately, had failed it. It was only after their list was depleted that the company hired a young man just out of school for the apprenticeship. The company couldn't discriminate against the lad because his uncle happened to be an assistant superintendent.

Ziggy asked for the list of those who flunked the test, and after a good deal of sparring the company read off their names and check numbers, which the union representative took down in long-hand, and asked for a few days to look into the entire matter. The company balked and accused the union of "procrastination." The industrial relations counsellor insisted the grievance must be settled that day (withdrawn) or immediately appealed to the fourth step of the grievance procedure. Fourth Step as most readers, by now, know, is no panacea, nor a referral to scholars, or specialists, or Holy Orders. Fourth Step removes the grievance from the hands of the local union and those who are closest to it, into the hands of the international union and those who are removed from the workplace and who always consider "the broader issues" rather than the worker with the grievance. But if the Company won't settle in third step, there's no other choice—except to give way, to withdraw, to surrender unconditionally.

Ziggy and his grievanceman checked all the names the company had submitted, and found four who said they had never applied, had no knowledge of the posting, and weren't interested in any apprenticeship. The other three had quit the plant months before the date the company said it had posted the notice. The suspicions that the Company wasn't telling the truth were overwhelming.

Weeks passed, and then months. With six hundred grievances waiting to be settled, it took almost a year before Ziggy's grievance came up on the fourth step agenda.

Ziggy wasn't at the hearing. Neither was his grievanceman. Nobody who actually worked in the plant was present at the fourth step hearing. The international union's staffman was there, and the company's superintendent of industrial relations was there. Each had one witness. For the company, the unbiased and unbossed general foreman of the electrical department. For the union, the appointed, salaried, chairman of the local union's grievance committee.

A half dozen grievances were on the agenda that day. Ziggy's was the final one to be considered. The others had been speeded through, agreed by both sides to have had "no merit." The company observed sarcastically that appealing so many chickenshit grievances to fourth step was the reason they were so far behind in settling grievances. The international staff-man was inclined to agree. The staffman turned to his witness and asked, "What do you know about this (Ziggy's) griev-ance?" To one who may never have had the experience of such a hearing, the witness' answer might have been a shock. But a mood and a method for the hearing had already been firmly set. Those local union people, you know, they have an eye on the local elections, and instead of telling the workers they don't have a real grievance, they throw everything into the lap of the international union. Well, the international staffman has the guts to withdraw those silly grievances.

The chairman of the grievance committee responding to the staffman's question, shook his head and answered he had per-sonally investigated Ziggy's grievance, and there was "nothing to it." He apologized for allowing the grievance to be put on the fourth step agenda.

That ended Ziggy's year-long fight for an apprenticeship he thought belonged to him. The company industrial relations superintendent reached into his briefcase and brought out a well-worn rubber stamp, pressed it to the inked pad, and slammed it hard onto the back of the grievance form. He signed it and then handed it to the staffman for his signature. It read, "Withdrawn by mutual consent of the union and the company."

By that time Ziggy had been promoted to a third class mill-wright, well on the road to become first class, and he doubted he would be willing to start at the bottom wage of an appren-tice, and spend four years to get a craft job in the plant that paid no more than his millwright job. He learned later that even after a four year apprenticeship in the electric shop of a steel mill, the building and construction unions wouldn't have recognized his journeyman status. He gave it up to a lost cause.

Chapter Fourteen

Invoking Article Twelve

Of all the rattle-trap cranes at Republic's steel plant in South Chicago, none could match the crane known, for mystic reasons never resolved by those who operated it, as *One Forty-Five -D*. The company purchased it in 1945 (that could be a clue) during the period when the federal government was picking up the tab for corporations producing war materiel. It had been owned and used by the Boston and Maine railroad for more than fifty years, and its re-location to the steel plant, according to the old-timers in the plant, was a shrewd business deal in which both parties made a magnificent contribution towards winning the war, besides making a decent profit.

The crane was eminently suited for changing the gigantic mill stands in the newly-built thirty-two inch mill, and to have waited for the construction of a new crane would have critically delayed steel production. Fifty years isn't too old for a crane kept in reasonable shape, and though it appeared unbecoming in the setting of a spanking new building and the most modern mill equipment of the time, with practiced handling at that time it accomplished its essential duties of changing stands, changing rolls, removing cobbles, replacing hot saws, and sundry maintenance of the mill, sure-footedly and without equivocation.

But now it was some thirty years later and *One Forty Five D* was noisy, jumpy and unpredictable. It often paid no attention whatsoever to the craneman. If the craneman centered the control on *STOP,* the crane might decide to travel another couple of feet before it obeyed. If the craneman carefully and precisely set the lift in motion for a slow, gradual pull, it would often leap up like a chicken that lost its head, or it might stand defiantly motionless, and cast an obscene gesture at the operator.

The bearings on the crane wheels were shot, the wheels themselves more egg-shaped than round, the shafts were bent, the rails bumpy, the electrical systems defective, and instead of gliding smoothly like a heavy-duty crane should, it would groan and hobble and jolt, and its cab would vibrate spasmodically as if it were having some kind of seizure. What this did for the cranemen, their guts, their backs, their ears, their heads, can be easily calculated.

And now it was getting worse by the day.

One of the operators, George, who was not Italian, said the noise was making him deaf, that when he went to see *The Godfather,* it was better for him when they were talking Italian—at least he could read the sub-titles.

(At a conference at Indiana University on April 17, 1971, Alexander Cohen, chief of the National Noise Study for the U.S. Public Health Service, said: "Noise abuses affect more people than any other form of environmental pollution," and asserted that 50,000 workers in Northwest Indiana "have substantial hearing disabilities" which, in most cases, are caused by long exposure to excessive noises on their job.

(A consultant to the United State Department of Labor has estimated that 60 to 70 percent of employees working in factories are exposed to dangerous levels of noise leading to loss of hearing.

(The Environmental Protection Agency published a notice in the *Federal Register* that said: "EPA has reviewed OSHA's [the federal government's Occupational Safety and

Health Administration] proposed standard for occupational exposure to noise, and in view of the best available data, has determined that the 90 dBA [the approved decibel standard of measuring noise] time-weighted level for an eight hour day does not adequately protect public health and welfare. EPA has identified a level of approximately 20 decibels below OSHA's 90 dBA as the safe level for protection against hearing loss . . . ").

Another operator on *One Forty Five D*, Matt, was being treated for a "bad back." He said it pained him some nights that he couldn't straighten out in bed. He also was in continuous friction with the family that he had the television sound up too high.

Leo, another craneman, said his nerves were shot because of the strain handling a crane that he never could predict, and he said he threw up his lunch almost every day.

There were five cranemen on *One Forty Five D*, and they all complained it wasn't safe, and that it was hurting their health. They had been saying it for years, and the company chose not to hear them. But now they said they really meant it . . . they had as much as they could take. Ascending the stairway to board the crane was like mounting the scaffold for the execution. To be altogether truthful, it wasn't only the fear of an accident that incensed the crane operators. Years on the crane without ever getting hurt develops resistance to such fears. And it wasn't a sudden awakening to their health problems, either. These grow so slowly the victims are hardly conscious they aren't enjoying good health, and there is hardly any great premonition of impending disaster. More to the point, was the gnawing resentment that they weren't being listened to, that they were viewed as outcasts, expendables, without the balls to confront the company.

After all those years, they decided on a most serious move: *to invoke Article Twelve* of the union contract.

Article Twelve reads: "If an employee shall believe there exists an unsafe condition . . . so that the Employee is in danger of injury . . . the Employee shall have the right . . . to be relieved from duty on the job in respect to which he has complained and to return to such job when the unsafe condition shall be remedied."

It's not as simple as it reads. It's a bewildering and uncoordinated procedure that can be disastrous to any worker who invokes it. In the thirty years it has been a part of the union contract, it has never been successful in correcting a single unsafe working condition—which accounts for the shift towards dependence on federal government intervention. Almost identical provisions are written into all union contracts, and the experience has been much the same.

Requesting to be relieved from duty until an unsafe condition shall be remedied runs into such hurdles as (1) is there *really* an unsafe condition? who says so? (2) what's to happen to the workers "relieved from duty" if there's no other work available? They can't be paid for staying home. (3) who shall decide if the unsafe condition has actually been remedied? (4) what happens to the other workers who aren't complaining and are willing to continue on the job?

There had been numerous instances at this plant where workers who invoked Article Twelve and requested to be relieved from duty on the job until an unsafe condition is remedied were "furloughed" for several weeks, during which they were not paid a penny and in the meantime other workers were assigned to and performed the same job. If the newly assigned workers had refused, they, too, could have been disciplined, even discharged. Although Article Twelve provides for the Company to reassign workers to another job when they invoke Article Twelve, it is the usual contention of the Company that no other job is available. Clearly, contract provisions on safety in the workplace are ambiguous and preposterous. It is hard to conceive of a more stumbling and humiliating procedure, pitting workers against each other, depriving them of any inclination or capacity to question a working condition they might consider unsafe, and giving the company almost limitless authority to decide what is safe or unsafe in the workplace and to punish workers who dissent.

At seven o'clock that morning, with only one hour remaining before the end of his turn, and while the mill was still rolling, the crane operator came down from his cab to the mill floor, and told the mill foreman that he and the other cranemen on *One Forty Five D* wanted to invoke Article Twelve.

The foreman pretended he didn't hear, or perhaps he didn't, as is common when the mind is crowded with instructions to be delivered. At any rate he said, "They want to change stands on the *intermediate* right away." This would require the craneman to get back in his crane cab and travel across the building, lift out the mill-stand in use, and replace it with another mill-stand that would roll steel bars of a different shape and dimension.

All night he had been changing stands, battling with his crane to do the job it was supposed to do, and making all kinds of adjustments and compromises with its incredibly irregular performance. He understood fully how important it was to change the stand, that the mill produce the steel the customer ordered. But he had gone over the whole matter in his mind, again and again, during the hostile night on *One Forty Five D,* whispering his lines to himself. He rehearsed it like Marlon Brando in a movie, and the foreman's answer wasn't in the script. It was supposed to be something like, "I'll call the superintendent," not anything about "changing mill stands."

The craneman started over, and repeated, "I want to invoke Article Twelve. This crane is unsafe." It is absolutely essential that the proper words be used— "I want to invoke Article Twelve"—otherwise the Company could misunderstand, and the issue, instead of *safety on the job,* becomes *refusing to work as directed,* and the employee may be sent home, disciplined for insubordination, or fired. The words make the issue. A misshapen word in such a charged situation, and not the misshapen wheels on the crane, or the incessant vibration of its cab, or the screeching noise far beyond OSHA's standard of 90 decibels, becomes the master key to undo a worker's pursuit of safety in the workplace.

The foreman took a deep breath and remained silent. His knowledge of the procedure wasn't practiced and he didn't want to goof. He sensed he had lost some authority, and decided to plead. Wait until the end of the turn and tell it to the superintendent. He'll be here in an hour. There'll be only a couple more lifts this morning. The roller is blowing five for the crane.

The craneman knew there was nothing to be gained from postponing the serious business at hand, and, besides, he was only one, with no right to make any changes in the line of action all of the cranemen on *One Forty Five D* had decided the night before. He had a grievance already written up and signed by all the cranemen, and it was burning a hole in his chest. He pulled it out of the inside of his shirt with an exaggerated flourish, like a carnival magician producing a dove, "Here, give this to your boss. We've made up our mind. This fuckin' crane ain't safe to run. We're invoking Article Twelve."

The grievance, printed in pencil on the regular form, simply said, "The cranemen on One Forty Five D invoke Article Twelve of the union contract on the grounds the crane is unsafe." It could have been written more persuasively and with more style, but there is no hard evidence or statistics to show that the language of a grievance has ever been a factor in getting a settlement in favor of the worker. On the contrary, it has sometimes happened that extensive description and argumentation in the statement of a grievance, like the statements of a prisoner in the dock, have been used against the grievant. Practiced union grievancemen have learned to limit the language of a union grievance to its bare essentials, and to be prepared with the facts and arguments in the various hearings of the grievance procedure.

The cranemen on *One Forty Five D* were well aware that the Company considered the invoking of Article Twelve on a par with a ship rebellion against its captain. But in the cranemen's view the ship was doomed, and invoking Article Twelve corresponded to the lowering of the life-boat, their last hope to reach shore.

It wasn't that the cranemen looked forward to a long skirmish with the company over the safety of the crane, or that they were encouraged by some mystical experience that took them beyond the rigid rules of the workplace. However, they sensed a subtle difference between their protest and all the others that had failed. They were bolstered by the intimate knowledge that all the cranemen on *One Forty Five D* were with one body and mind, and they had a comfortable feeling, too, derived more out of instinct than anything spoken or pledged, that the other two hundred cranemen in the plant would back them.

And, according to their account, it was hardly a surprise that at eight o'clock, when the day-turn craneman arrived and both the day and night-turn cranemen stood in position at the foot of the stairway, and neither made a move to ascend the crane, that the superintendent immediately read the message, and told them *One Forty Five D* was going down for repairs that morning, and that the cranemen were to be transferred to other cranes throughout the plant. There was no mention of Article Twelve or the grievance. And it would be like rubbing the company's nose in the dirt to suggest that invoking Article Twelve, or the heretical manner of the cranemen had forced the issue.

When the cranemen returned from their temporary duty in other parts of the plant, they were elated over the smooth operation of the totally revamped *One Forty Five D*. It was now like a well-tuned instrument. It responded to the lightest touch of their skilled fingers and hands. Their only regret was that they had waited so long, that they had listened too well to those who had experienced terror and hopelessness in plodding through the thorny grievance process. They showed the company and the union a surer and simpler way.

Of course, the repairs couldn't reverse the damage already done to the cranemen's health. Of the four, Leo took an early retirement after an operation on his back. George wears a hearing aid. Matt and Joe are being treated for undiagnosed ailments. They're not sure what's wrong. "The doctors don't tell you."

A recent landmark civil suit, in whicn John Shoop, a retired steelworker from the U.S. Steel plant at Clairton, Pennsylvania, claimed his hearing was impaired by the noise in the mill, resulted in an award of $30,000 in damages. Not a financial windfall, or a solution available to many workers. But one can't resist the whimsical theory that if a fair and just jury award were made to all the millions of victims of occupational accidents and diseases, it would result in a more far-reaching distribution of the nation's wealth than ever dreamed by Utopians.

Chapter Fifteen

The Toothless Tiger in
the Coke Plant

For a brief period immediately following the enactment of the Occupational Safety and Health Act of 1970 (a federal law to establish, investigate, monitor and enforce safety and health standards in the workplace, and familiarly called OSHA), management people at the plant level (foremen, supervisors, superintendents and assistants) carried on as if the armies of treason had overrun the land, and that "management's right to manage" had been converted to a cardinal sin. Engaged as they are in the daily routines and pressures of the workplace, the lower ranks of management, often, even more than the workers, are cordoned off from political events, except for what is presented to them by their superiors through conferences, bulletins, operations meetings, trade papers. The political candidates they support, like the lodges and orders they join, the charities and causes they contribute to, the communities they live in, the style and locale of their vacations, are all predictable, and conform to a conscious discipline. In many workplaces, as soon as, and sometimes before, an employee is tapped for a management position, he is recruited into the Masonic order or the Knights of Columbus. Though gifted in matters of production, maintenance, scheduling, labor discipline and plant regulations, they have, generally, a simplistic view of politics and easily fit into the political groupings of the right wing.

The debates, hearings, testimony, and voting in the United States Congress which resulted in the enactment of OSHA escaped the notice of the lower echelons of management, and it wasn't until they were advised by higher-ups that they could be vulnerable as possible violaters of OSHA that they became aroused. Many of them had paranoiac fantasies of being summonsed, shoved into a wooden chair under hot klieg lights, and rubber-hosed into confessing all sorts of fictitious safety violations. It was all so much more business-like when state factory inspectors, practical people, some their personal friends, neighbors and lodge brothers, made their once-a-year visit to the plant, and after shooting the breeze for an hour or so in the gatehouse, would accept an invitation to go out for a drink.

OSHA? OSHA? Was this some kind of revenge, an anti-business creation, a pinko plot to take control of industry?

At plant safety meetings with employees, at union-management conferences, at industrial relations hearings, wherever plant supervision communicated with its workers, there were fretful warnings of reprisals. If OSHA snoopers gave them a hard time and closed down any operations or imposed any fines against the company, they, the workers, would be the losers. We're gonna have to crack down. Any employee caught working unsafe, will be sent home. Period. Any employee without his goggles on at all times—even at lunch—will be sent home. Period. Safety locks, leggings, safety belts, any safety equipment the company issues must be on the employee at all times. This is a two-way street. Period. A shrill theme of workers and management uniting against OSHA was sounded in the workplaces throughout the land.

And many workers, unaware of the intent of OSHA, could easily believe that, having come from Washington, it was probably a danger to them. At a steel union conference on safety and health held in Pittsburgh on November 3, 1975, a full five years after OSHA became law, a delegate, a safety committeeman, said: "I'd tell you my name, but I'd lose my job. Both the company and the union are against calling in the government. I'm in the middle. What good does it do to shut them down?" The international union, which had lobbied more vigorously for OSHA than any other labor union, replied that "these are hardly simple questions that can be answered with a yes or no." (*Steel Labor,* December, 1975)

Labor union officialdom, from the very beginning was, and remains, less than enthusiastic about OSHA, not, primarily, because of its half-hearted and ambiguous provisions, but out of a firmly-established positon that collective bargaining can handle safety and health in the workplace better than government. Labor's aloofness towards the Civil Rights Act, environmental control, women's rights, or any legislation that might under-cut the union-management role comes from the same source. It helps account for the AFL-CIO's acquiescence to an utterly absurd federal minimum wage standard. Wage rates must be established through collective bargaining and not by legislation.

Issues of safety and health in the workplace continue to be handled through the grievance procedures as provided in union contracts, and OSHA, like so many government boards, is usually by-passed as a matter of policy.

It's not only a matter of Labor's attitudes towards OSHA, but OSHA itself doesn't come across as reliable about safety in the workplace. It doesn't provide the personnel to do the job. It doesn't punish offenders. It hedges and shifts on standards. It goes easy on the companies.

The deputy assistant secretary of Labor, Howard T. Schulte, in his report in the June 13, 1974 issue of the *Occupational Safety and Health Reporter,* said:

"Currently there are 1,500 state inspectors and 900 federal compliance officers covering the 4.1 million workplaces in the nation. (Eighty-seven percent of the workplaces in the nation are not covered by the Act, exempted under the rules. These are the smaller workplaces, accounting for twenty per cent of the nation's work force.) With that number of inspectors it would take ten to twelve years to inspect all the workplaces once."

If the lower ranks of management mis-read OSHA and over-reacted, and labor leaders and workers had their doubts, sophisticated corporate leaders took it in their stride and didn't become terrified by OSHA. The leaders of the AFL-CIO must be extremely naive to believe "the administration of OSHA has frightened employers. They don't understand the act or the standards they are required to meet." (From Report adopted by the AFL-CIO Executive Council at its February 1975 meeting.)

Employers aren't in the least frightened, and they *do* understand. They understand that OSHA is a toothless tiger that couldn't hurt a mouse. That the very worst an average large employer could expect is an inspection once in ten or twelve years. The big-time polluters, the most ferocious spoilers of the environment and health, seem confident they have the government and the union under control.

When a federal environmental agency objected to the daily discharge of 67,000 tons of taconite waste into Lake Superior, where was OSHA?

The Reserve Mining Company's taconite plants, owned jointly by Republic Steel and Armco Steel at Silver Bay, Minnesota, were ordered by the U.S. District Court to close because the wastes being dumped into Lake Superior were endangering the health of the entire community which used the water from this lake for drinking. The evidence showed that the taconite "tailings" contained asbestos fibers that are linked to cancer.

Then, what happened? Did the frightened employers accept the court's ruling in earnestness and good faith? It wasn't quite that way. The mining company and the steel companies, providers of economic security, noted that the judge's ruling would mean the loss of 3000 miners' jobs, and the steel companies which depend on the taconite from these mines for the manufacture of iron and steel, would be compelled to close many of its operations. The number of jobs that would be lost snow-balled fantastically to 100,000.

"This whole thing just opened up a huge can of worms," said the Republic Steel spokesman, and added that "the judge didn't look beyond the end of his nose" in ordering the taconite operations closed.

The Steelworkers Union, although it is committed to safe drinking water and protection of its members from asbestosis, went into court on the side of the companies, to have the district court's order over-ruled. After six years of litigation, and after the release of the U.S. Department of Health, Education and Welfare estimate that at least 100,000 workers die each year from occupational diseases which are caused by chemicals such as asbestos, the Supreme Court of the United States ruled that it would allow the Reserve Mining Company "a reasonable time" to stop discharging wastes into Lake Superior and into the air. Two years after the Supreme Court ruling the companies continue to dump taconite "tailings" linked to cancer into the lake.

In a similar setting, the U. S. Steel plant in Gary, Indiana was ordered to shut down one of its open hearth furnaces because of its emission of harmful pollutants. The steel company had not responded to repeated warnings from the environmental agency, and after two six-month extensions and there was no move of any kind made by the company, it was finally ordered shut down. In this conflict, a newly elected steelworkers union district director, Ed Sadlowski, who was at odds with the international union's accomodation to industry pollution, and was thoroughly fed up with OSHA, asserted that the acid test of OSHA was how it protected the safety and health of the workers and their communities. The open hearth furnace was closed down. The corporation spends millions in public relations to convince the public that in the battle for ecology it's a toss-up between U.S. Steel and the Izaak Walton League.

So, who's afraid of OSHA?

Clyde Davis, a rank and file worker from the coke department at Republic Steel's South Chicago plant, wrote a letter to OSHA, Chicago office. He told OSHA that several grievances had been filed protesting polluted conditions in the coke plant, but nothing had been done. He told OSHA it was dangerous to his health, and he wanted them to investigate. And then he waited.

Eugene Pughsley, the local union grievanceman in the coke plant, sat down, after a day in the coke plant, and, in the cool of the night, penciled a letter to the local union newspaper: "I remember," he wrote, "the last day of work for Ernest James in the coke plant. We were riding on the bus, going home, back in April of 1974. He was sad. Not because he was dying of cancer, but because the company had given him a clean bill of health on his last physical check-up, required by OSHA He said he went to his own doctor a few weeks later because he was sick. His doctor told him he was dying of cancer. James mentioned to me that he had given the best years of his life to the company, and the company gave him a false report on his physical examination.

"The coke plant employees are frightened after seeing so many of our men dying before or soon after retiring. We all realize that one of these days we are all going to die, but does it have to be at such a rapid pace as at the coke plant?"

A study of health records of 100,000 steelworkers at seventeen plants that began in 1962, published by the U. S. Department of Labor in 1974, says:

" . . . . Coke workers as a group are two and one half times more likely to die of lung cancer than steelworkers who do not work in coke plants."

" . . . . After five years on the job (in the coke plant) the lung cancer rate rises to three and one-half times the normal rate."

" . . . . For workers on top of the coke batteries with five years on the job, the death rate is ten times higher than normal."

Pughsley, the local grievanceman, wasn't exaggerating.

It is agreed by all coke plant workers that the principal source of exposure is the coal dust and gases that leak from the coke ovens when they are being "charged." The conditions are worsened when the ovens are in poor condition, when the doors don't fit tight, and when the employees are being pushed and aren't allowed "spell time" to get some fresh outside air.

Certainly, if there ever was an over-ripe delinquency in which OSHA might easily sink its teeth, the coke plant was a perfect example. It could order the steel company, could it not, to clean up its coke plant, to repair the doors, and to change its method of charging, as is done in some other plants, which would eliminate the gas and dust. It is called "stage charging," where coal is emptied from a larry-car into the coke oven in three seperate steps, rather than all at once. It takes more time, and increases the need for more workers, but it reduces the escape of gas and dust by ninety percent.

OSHA, in response to Clyde Davis' complaint, sent its investigators to the Republic Steel plant, and spent a full day at the coke plant. They talked to workers and supervisors. They made tests with different instruments the workers had never seen before. They made extensive notes on yellow pads, like lawyers use, and they shook their heads, obviously distressed by conditions. As they left the plant, one of the investigators raised his arm in a *Black power salute,* augered as a good omen by the coke plant workers.

Five month's later, OSHA sent a written report to the Company and to the union. That report earned them the title of "the toothless tiger."

"There is no solution, engineering-wise, to correct the pollution condition in this coke plant area," said the report, and it recommended that employees in the **coke** plant wear respirators.

Respirators in steel plants are similar to those used in coal mines, and are designed to protect against dust, not gas. Smoke and fumes from the coke ovens get inside the respirators and the workers can't breathe. It is physically impossible to wear the dust respirator for any length of time without becoming dizzy from lack of oxygen.

The company and the union, once more finding a solution in collective bargaining, negotiated an agreement to ignore the OSHA recommendation—it wasn't an order—and that the wearing of respirators in the coke plant would be "voluntary." Small victories, too, must be appreciated.

Since that time, in October 1976, OSHA handed down its long-awaited standard which sets "permissible levels" of exposure to coke oven fumes. The standard states that "workers exposure will be limited to 150 micrograms of benzine-fraction of total particulate matter of cubic meter of air averaged over an eight-hour period." Dr. Morton Corn, Assistant Secretary of Labor acknowledged that there was no "safe level" of exposure. But the Labor Department, with toothless warnings to industry and labor about the "economic feasibility" of cleaning up the coke ovens, gave the companies four more years, until January 20, 1980, to meet the OSHA standard.

And yet industrial management still longs for those good old days when factory inspection was in the hands of people who knew how to get along with industry, instead of rampaging through the workplace like a blood-hungry tiger.

Chapter Sixteen

The Fingers, Arms, Legs, Balls, and Carcasses of Blue Collar Workers Still Come at Bargain Prices

Folklore and fact combine to support a curiously romantic notion that, like *Joe Magarac,* the legendary steelworker who ended up as a cinder in a crucible of steel, blue collar workers, typically, shut their eyes to all premonitions or warnings of danger in the workplace, and, as part of their fate and fortune —conceivably as a challenge to their machismo—anticipate or even flirt with a similarly grim end to their every workday. The perpetrators of these myths could be quite easily traced to employers and directors of blue collar workers, and to what amounts to a quarantine which painstakingly restricts the public from any contacts with the insides of the workplaces of America. These restrictions are enforced even to prohibit workers within their own regular places of employment from visiting other areas of the plant to see what goes on. A worker caught "Away from his work area" can be disciplined or fired.

That the public thirsts for knowledge of what goes on in the workplace seems to be confirmed by the 200,000 citizens who lined up over a ten day period in July, 1976, at the U.S. Steel plant in Gary, Indiana, in response to the company's announcement of a guided bicentennial tour through the plant.

The company was prepared for only a fraction of them, and thousands were turned away.

Of course, visitors performing a bicentennial obligation to their Founding Fathers don't discover much that's true in a guided tour which is heavily laced with self-serving propaganda about the company's concerns and expenditures for the safety and health of its employees, and being told, repeatedly, that "the average American is safer at the workplace than he is at home." But there are other, more reliable, simpler ways to ascertain that the estimated 100,000 American workers destroyed each year by industrial accidents and occupational diseases probably did not pull a *Joe Magarac* and arrange their own self-destruction. They were innocent victims, bagged and snared in the cunning violence of the workplace.

There's no denying that blue collar workers, generally speaking, aren't diligent in observing the safety rules of the workplace. They are quite willing to take the normal risks of working, but they regard most of the safety rules as frivolous, unreal, as unworkable nuisances purposely inflicted on workers to bug them and blame them if they should get hurt. A worker injured on the job is immediately third-degreed with such questions as, did you have your safety goggles on? where was your safety-lock? were you wearing your hard-hat? were you out of your work-area? though none of these, by the wildest imagination, could have any bearing on the causes of the accident, and have as their purpose to represent the accident as personal, caused by the worker's defiance of company safety rules.

Workers are insulted by the extravagant claims of management such as, for one example, that the wearing of a hard-hat in a crane-cab, or in a mill-pulpit, or on an assembly-line, or in most work areas in the plants, is a valid or worthwhile protection against head injuries. Except for a few industries and jobs, the ridiculous doctrine of gate-house to gate-house or locker-room to locker-room wearing of the hard-hat has about the same relevance to industrial and occupational safety as the army chaplain's soothing story about the infantry soldier whose life was spared when an enemy bullet was stopped by the Bible he carried in his shirt pocket, has to the relevance of war. There are many such fables and spiritual movements behind industry's smug, self-serving, concocted safety programs. (Incidentally, industry's safety directors are listened to by production managers about as closely as battle commanders listen to army chaplains.)

The real causes of most accidents in the workplace are working conditions over which the workers have no control, and no amount of company preaching, chewing out workers at safety meetings, propaganda posters at the gate-house, changing styles of safety shoes or goggles, can change these conditions. The company short-cuts to faster production, the make-do equipment and temporary repairs to last through the day, the postponing of the closing down of an unsafe operation, the unceasing nerve-wracking pressure on workers for greater production, the emission of sickening and dangerous fumes and chemicals, the extremes of heat and cold—these are the hazards of the workplace that can wound, disable or kill.

The guided tour through an industrial plant gives little worthwhile information about how and why 100,000 workers in the United States are wiped out each year in the workplace. A far better method is to examine the grievances and complaints of workers in the workplace registering their protest against unsafe working conditions, and how the company managements respond to these grievances and complaints. More can be learned from the simple hard fact that in a quite typical plant of five thousand employees on the south side of Chicago (Republic Steel)—almost any other workplace in any other industry in any other community, not excluding even the bicentennial showplace in Gary, Indiana, could be selected, and the experience would be quite the same—the workers in a normal year file over two hundred written safety grievances which involve roughly twenty five hundred employees, or half the workers, in the plant. And there are another

couple of hundred unrecorded, verbal, complaints, all protesting unsafe working conditions in the plant, all presented by
blue collar workers who don't in the least aspire to the charis-
ma of *Joe Magarac*. They believe profoundly that they have
the right to punch out at the end of their turn with all their
limbs and organs intact. Nationwide, there are roughly a
hundred thousand safety grievances filed yearly.

A lengthy strike in 1974 against the Gould Battery plant in
Trenton, New Jersey, conducted by the independent and un-
affiliated United Electrical, Radio and Machine Workers Union (UE) over the issue of inadequate protection of the workers from lead poisoning, is another simple hard fact of what
blue collar workers feel about safety in the workplace. This
strike received extraordinary attention from the media, not
because the issue was a unique one—the very same conditions
prevail in numerous plants—but because it was something of
a revelation that blue collar workers would take such a positive stand and pay so high a price, in terms of loss of wages,
for safety in their workplace.

If the conservative, business-minded, tough, old leadership
of the labor movement could, for a moment only, slack up its
anxiety over productivity and the state of the market, and
would allow the workers in the plants, no, not support or en-
couragement, but only the bare permission to conduct a fair
fight for their rights to a safe workplace, there would be
hundreds and hundreds of such actions all over the country,
and that would go a long way, don't you think, in ending the
nightmare of 100,000 deaths and 3,000,000 "recordable occupational injuries and illnesses" which are reported in the 1973
President's Report on Occupational Safety and Health. This
doesn't imply a request for a kind of guerilla warfare or an-
archy in the workplace. Blue collar workers are not guinea
pigs to be used to prove a social or political theory. With a few
exceptions that stand out like bumps on a log, the workers are
in the plants to make their living, and, ordinarily, they can't
afford to lose even a day from work. Labor leaders who fear

that workers don't have enough of a stake in their workplaces to be trusted with the right to strike over unsafe working conditions are far removed from the realities of the work world.

International unions negotiate contracts that set up unworkable procedures permitting workers to file grievances wherever the company violates its pledge "to make reasonable provisions for the safety and health of its employees," (the wording in most labor agreements). And, since "reasonableness" cannot be rushed, safety grievances under collective bargaining agreements take years to be settled. Sometimes after it is too late. Only rarely does the company give in. Usually, after the long delays, the workers become accustomed to the condition they are protesting, and the issue drifts. Workers attempting to protest more vigorously than filing a grievance risk serious reprisals from both management and the union.

Not industry, not government, not the official labor movement can escape blame for the corrupt and ruthless game in which workers' safety and health has been manipulated and sacrificed. Whatever progress has been made over the years in providing a safer workplace has been the scanty and bitter fruit of workers' rank and file rebellion, aided, on occasion, as in the coal fields, by mavericks within the scientific and medical communities. Courageous coal miners and their friends fought for years for protection against the "black lung disease" and were confronted by a united front of coal operators and international union officials. The miners won their battle, at least partially, by replacing their union leadership with one that supported their fight for mine safety. Though this is an example of a rare victory, it is not by any means a rare example of industry-government-union collaboration against rank and file workers trying to improve safety and health standards in the workplace.

In our free, profit-oriented society, almost anyone who has the money can hire a lawyer, go into court, and sue for damages. But not for the damages, no matter how conspicuous or crippling, which industry may inflict on the limbs and organs of its workers. In such circumstances, there were established special laws and special rules that plainly define and control the inferior status of industrial workers, and protect the superior status of the employers. Every state in the union enacted a Workmen's Compensation Law (currently being re-named in several states to delete its sexist title, but not its class bias). The laws set the cash benefits workers may collect from their employers in the event of their disablement from an industrial accident or disease. The laws lay down a schedule of prices, like the OPA posted in retail markets during World War II, for arms, legs, eyes, ears, genitals, the whole carcass of a worker. Though employers often complain, and state legislators usually listen, that the prices are set too high, deep-down they know they're getting the biggest bargain in town. Moreover, the Workmen's Compensation laws send out dark, under-the-counter, signals to industry that it can be cheaper to overlook an unsafe or unhealthful condition in the workplace—a leaking oven in a coke plant, a defective switch on a mill crane, a worn pump in an oil refinery, a malfunctioning conveyor in an auto plant, a stopped-up ventilating system in any of the dusty trades, the rash experimentation with toxic chemicals to meet the competitive demands of the market— even if it may result in human disfigurement, disablement, diseases or death. (If this seems like a fuzzy re-run of nineteenth century anti-capitalist literature, it may be because our society has become so thoroughly toughened to accept violence of all descriptions, or because of the tremendous difficulties in comprehending the new, often deliberately hidden, industrial hazards created, since World War II, by new industrial processes, and sharply stepped-up competitive practices throughout the world.)

The state of Illinois, with one of the more generous Workmen's Compensation laws, currently (1976) provides the following benefits for losses to a married worker with two children:

Ring finger—25 weekly installments totalling $2222.50.
Little finger—20 weekly installments totalling $1,778.
Hand—190 weekly installments totalling $16,891.
Arm—235 weekly installments totalling $20,891.50.
Leg—200 weekly installments totalling $17,780.
Testicle—one testicle, 50 weekly installments totalling $4,445; two testicles—150 weekly installments totalling $13,335.
Death—the spouse receives two-thirds of the workers weekly wage for life or until remarriage. If there is no spouse, the beneficiary receives two years of benefits, totalling $10,608.

Several economically more backward states, to lure industry to its territory, offer prospective employers, in addition to tax breaks, lower workmen's compensation rates in the event of industrial accidents and diseases. In Oklahoma a worker disabled by a job-related injury gets a paltry $50 a week, while in Michigan, with five dependents, it's a lavish $144.

No part of the worker's body is un-priced, and the total price of the entire carcass is set at rock-bottom. As with an automobile, the whole is priced much less than the sum of its parts. Auto insurance companies, dealing in plastics and steel, can afford to be more straightforward than industry dealing with humans, and the insurance companies freely confess they prefer "totals" to partial wrecks. A 1976 study of automobile-repair costs by the American Mutual Insurance Alliance found that it costs more to repair damages to only one-fourth of the car's parts than to buy a new automobile. The same equation is adhered to by workmen's compensation laws for the mutilated bodies of workers. "Totals" are cheaper, no matter how you cut it.

With all that, a shrewd employer, possessed of virtuosity and driven by the codes of a bustling black market, knows how to get special discounts on the legal rate. With the right combination of sweet talk, and mean innuendos, an injured worker can't easily risk turning down a company offer. According to the Industrial Commission of Illinois, only seven percent of injured workers receive as much benefits as the minimum which the Workmen's Compensation law lists as a fair settlement. Most workers fear there may be reprisals from the employer if they turn down the reduced settlement. The alternative of appealing to the industrial commission isn't very encouraging. It's not like a trial by your peers. The hearing officers are political appointees, friends of the employer's attorneys and doctors, and it could take a year to get a hearing. In the meantime there's no money coming in. At the hearings, the company doctors produce medical records and arguments that nobody can understand, and somehow they manage to make a malingerer and a liar out of an injured worker. Best to take the money. A bird in the hand is worth two in the bush.

(OSHA provides twenty steps through which industry can appeal, in order, as OSHA puts it, "to guarantee due process of law." But an injured worker who feels his leg has been auctioned off too cheaply, has no way to appeal from a decision of the industrial commission.)

In the three score years, since the state of Wisconsin, inspired by its liberal state university, passed the first workmen's compensation bill, (subsequently followed by the other states) these laws continue to be acclaimed by labor leaders, social workers, philanthropists, economists, clergy, as the crowning achievement of social statesmanship. And nowhere, at no time, in that sixty some years of changes in social attitudes, has anyone heard a loud clear voice of a civil libertarian, a populist legislator, a spiritual advisor, a social humanist, a woman's rights group, denounce or seek to change the workmen's compensation laws—to give the blue collar worker the same or equal right to collect damages to their bodies as a passenger in an airplane or automobile accident, or a guest hurt at a country club or a ski-resort.

To anyone who attended the coroner's inquest in the fatal accident of James Dobrzeniecki and Chester Mangan, killed in the melt shop at Republic Steel's south Chicago plant on

December 6, 1967, it is so simply and outrageously unjust.

This is the way Charley Ramanna, a first helper on the open-hearth furnace saw the accident (though he wasn't given the opportunity to tell it at the hearing):

"The number three door on the Number Three Open Hearth furnace was scheduled to be changed because of the wear of the refractory lining. But it was decided to wait, and change the door *after one more heat* was tapped. (That's the way it always is: one more heat.)

"About 1:05 P.M. a noise that sounded like escaping steam was heard, and the door exploded. The front section, weighing about 3000 pounds, was hurled across the charging floor, and struck the charging car hot rails opposite the furnace. A one hundred and seventy five foot welded section of the hot rails was dislodged and fell, striking Dobrzeniecki and Mengan."

The union safety steward, Jim Browne, made these observations:

"(1) There were no safety plugs on the furnace doors of Number Three Open Hearth. (2) The charging car rails weren't bolted down. (3) The furnace door should have been changed earlier, before it had worn so badly. These corrections were made *after* the accident."

The workers who came to the coroner's inquest never had the chance to tell their story. The coroner, politely enough, wasn't interested. He explained that the jury had only to decide whether the deaths were due to accident, suicide, murder, or any other criminal activity. And what about the unsafe conditions the workers wished to talk about? Not germane . . . Irrelevant . . . Inconsequential . . . Etcetera . . . Etcetera.

In France, early last year, in the village of Vendin-le-Vieil a workman was killed in a coal-tar processing plant, and upon the disclosure that the company had knowingly ignored unsafe conditions in the plant, the plant manager was arrested on a charge of manslaughter. Nothing like that has ever happened in the United States.

James Dobrzeniecki's sister came to the hearing and asked to be heard. One might think, if it were only out of reverence for the human spirit, and in the absence of any other trace of sentimentality in the hearing that her request might have been granted. This isn't a town meeting, said a company spokesman. She pleaded, can't I say just a few words? The coroner said we have a full schedule and there isn't enough time.

She wrote what she planned to say and sent it to the local union editor:

"Why on December 6 was the life of my brother snuffed out? He was only 27 years old. He was eager for life and adventure. He was educated and willing to work. He was a human being, created by God, unique in his own individual way. He was a devoted son, a helpful brother, a loving husband and father.

"Why was his wife notified of his death in such a cruel and heartless way. Why did one man hold back tears, and another joke about it?

"Why was his mother informed of her son's death by a nameless radio announcer, blaring the news of an explosion at Republic Steel?

"Why was his bereaved family left suspended, information withheld, technicalities not fully explained, assistance not offered?

"Why hadn't the door of the furnace been changed before the event, as it should have been? Was that mound of molten steel so important?

"Why wasn't my brother warned of impending danger, as he walked so innocently by the furnace?

"Why are the lives of others jeopardized? Was it to keep production at an all time high?

"Why did the door explode? Why did it fly so high?

"Why did so many fail to come to the inquest and speak their minds? Why weren't the families told what to expect, so as to prepare themselves for the proceedings? Why were the proceedings rushed, and the voices of the families squelched when they wanted their questions answered?

"Why did some high ranking officials pretend to comfort with one hand, while picking apart with the other? Why so utterly false with promise? Why so blind to sorrow and anguish, no insight into personal feelings and misery brought into our lives by neglect and carelessness? Why so greedy? No amount of money can bring back our loved ones, or mend our broken hearts."

The letter was signed by Mrs. Geraldine Guiney. It was printed, without comment, in the local union paper.

Well-bred sophisticates who have no conception or feeling at all about blue collar workers may scoff at such reports of "good guys" and "bad guys" in the workplace. They may consider them naive, doctrinnaire, or uncouth. But, as Bertolt Brecht poetized *(War Primer)* as part of his struggle against the Nazis:

If ordinary people don't think
about being ordinary
They will never rise.

Epilogue

In these present days, often classified as a post-McCarthyite euphoria, when disobedient and defenseless citizens are no longer hauled before government or private investigating committees to be bullied and accused of dangerous thoughts, and when, curiously enough, "radical" anti-establishment magazines and studies sniff around for, and receive, enabling subsidies from wealthy foundations, the liberal and intellectual community is engaging in a popular post-mortem on the effects of McCarthyism on careers and institutions in America. Symposiums, films, banquets, victory celebrations and reunions of once-blacklisted but now rehabilitated artists, writers, entertainers, television and Hollywood personalities, elatedly lay to rest the stinking corpse of the 1950s, and salute the new liberation, and, not extraneously, their own newly restored status.

But, as is often the case in such victory-flushed ceremonies, due to poor planning, or poor understanding, or vanity, the absentees, the uninvited, the names that never got on the guest-list, are more interesting than those who show. *No places are set at the table for the blue collar worker.*

To the blue collar worker, psychological terror, economic threats, anti-labor laws, police brutality—all the basic ingredients of McCarthyism—have been every-day fare, before, during, and since Senator Joseph McCarthy was officially crowned and then silenced. This is plainly visible in the simple structure of the workplace. In terms of the working conditions, the insecurity, the fear, the disciplines, restrictions, and fundamental relations between employer and employee, it's clear that Senator McCarthy didn't invent McCarthyism. Equal, if not superior rights belong to several generations of familiar political and industrial figures at whose knee McCarthy learned his catechism of terror. Alongside such highly distinguished names (and this will make some readers uncomfortable) as George Pullman, Henry Frick, John D. Rockefeller, Elbert Gary, Thomas Girdler, Henry Ford, Richard Nixon—an incredibly long and mean list of scoundrels, professionals in the history of violence against workers and popular rights—Senator Joseph McCarthy hardly rates.

In an analytical study of repression in the United States, is it valid, or is it purely a private exercise of the mind, to equate the burning of the tent-colony of the Colorado Fuel and Iron Company's striking miners in 1914, which killed thirty-three men, women and children, with, let us say, the ousting of Professor Scott Nearing from his university chair for speaking out against World War I? Or, to compare the killing of ten steelworkers and wounding one hundred during a 1937 strike at Republic Steel in South Chicago (known as the Memorial Day Massacre), with, let us say, the blacklisting of a television commentator. Certainly, in both instances, the use of terror to exact obedience to the state is indefensibly villainous. And in both instances the terror originated from, and reflected, the same social arrangement. Though it might appear indecent to measure degrees of terror, the point has to be made that because the black-listed intellectuals have a superior sense of public relations, and have a wider and more influential following, and are so witty and entertaining, their bouts with McCarthyism receive top billing, while the blue collar workers' struggle for basic rights is largely ignored.

How can one be so innocent to believe that in the critical

post-war period during which capitalism in the United States irrationally feared the challenge of the socialist nations of Europe and Asia, that McCarthyite repression was aimed exclusively, or even principally, at avant-garde poets, obscure philosophers, night-club entertainers, or Marxist clerks. Of course, there were many advantages to be gained by creating a climate of witch-hunting and political plots. Graham Greene, in an address upon receiving a Shakespeare prize, said, "It has always been in the interests of the State to poison the psychological wells, to encourage cat-calls, to restrict human sympathy. It makes government easier when the people shout Gallilean, Papist, Fascist, Communist." But, it should be obvious that the establishment in the United States was then, and is now, much more deeply and fundamentally concerned with happenings in the workplaces, where the nation's ability to win any cold war would be finally decided, rather than what was happening in the studios.

It is not a personal question, nor one of vanity or wounded pride, or because it's required to love liberals less in order to love blue collar workers more, but, one must ask, who was damaged more by Joe McCarthy's cat-calls and terror? The colorful, black-listed, Hollywood writer, or the homely, obscure, blue collar workers, who like ingots in a steel mill or stock in an auto plant, are known by a number? And, if it is thought through logically and historically, not to depreciate the spirit of those brave liberals who defied McCarthy, who was the more despised target? Who were they most interested in nailing?

Who, other than workers, had their organizations under such regular surveillance, as if they were dangerous prisoners plotting a break-out? Police departments in a hundred cities maintain "labor details", also known as "red squads" with incredible armies of operatives to infiltrate and spy on labor organizations. Accountants, or professionals, or lawyers, or business executives' organizations aren't bothered by police watches—only workers.

Here we are talking, not of the 1877 days of the Molly Maguires or the 1937 days of Little Steel, but of the immediate present. Of the Taft-Hartley Law passed in 1947 (characterized then by Miners' Union president John L. Lewis as "the first, ugly, savage thrust of Fascism in America") under which any union that elected an officer that refused to bow to the McCarthy definition of "loyalty" would be outlawed, and non-conforming unions were denied the right of bargaining for its members in the plants. It worked so well that the loyalty oaths were extended by McCarthy's proteges to cover employees in city, state and federal government, to the university, publishing and entertainment world.

It was under that same spell of repression and witchcraft, in 1949, that eleven international unions of more than two million members in plants, factories, ships, warehouses, were charged with "masquerading as labor unions" and were expelled from the CIO, leaving its workers stranded, and laying the groundwork for the destruction of the CIO.

In the workplaces and in the trade unions, the gruesome slogans and style of McCarthyism have deep roots which have not yet been uprooted.

Just because the climate has seemingly changed so much for liberals and intellectuals, it should not screen out the intimidation, the black-listing, the red-baiting, the cat-calling, the totalitarian practices that still pervade the workplace.

It is often easy to misjudge the early signs of social change. It is easy to be silent about the blue collar workers, who are far down at the bottom of the social heap. And, for those whose profession it is to govern the state, the temptations have always been to be concerned only with its top surface layers, the rich, the educated, the powerful. But sooner or later the world will shift. And the stirring may well shake the stratified hierarchy of the workplace, and produce an industrial environment from which there will emerge workingclass heroes to blow the whistle on "scoundrel time" for all America.